Salmon Coast To Coast

Salmon Coast To Coast

Complete Angler's Library®
North American Fishing Club
Minneapolis, Minnesota

Salmon Coast To Coast

Copyright © 1991, North American Fishing Club

Library of Congress Catalog Card Number 91-66690
ISBN 0-914697-43-9

Printed in U.S.A.
      6   7   8   9

Contents

Acknowledgments

The North American Fishing Club would like to thank everyone who made this book possible.

Wildlife artist Virgil Beck created the cover art; artists David Rottinghaus and John A. (Buzz) Buczynski created illustrations. Du Pont Company's Fishing Products Group and L&S Bait Company, Inc. contributed additional artwork. Photographs were provided by the authors. Buzz Ramsey, Doug Wilson, Ed Park, Lue Park, Paul DeMarchi and Debra Podurgiel contributed additional photos.

A special thanks to the fishing club's publication staff for their efforts to complete this book: Editor and Publisher Mark LaBarbera, Managing Editor Steve Pennaz, Managing Editor Ron Larsen, Associate Editor Colleen Ferguson and Art Director Dean Peters. Thanks also to Vice President of Product Marketing Mike Vail, Marketing Manager Cal Franklin and Marketing Project Coordinator Laura Resnik.

About The Authors

Born in Germany's Black Forest region in 1946, George Gruenefeld arrived in Canada at the tender age of seven and felt right at home in the rolling hills of the Canadian Shield, an area he has crossed and recrossed countless times looking for angling adventures.

George estimates that he spends upwards of 100 days a year on the water, and wishes he could devote even more time to explore new frontiers.

His travels have taken him to all corners of North America. George has fished for bonefish and tarpon in the Gulf of Mexico, arctic char in the cold waters of the North, bluefin tuna off the Atlantic coast, marlin off the Pacific coast, Atlantic salmon in eastern coastal waters and Pacific salmon in Western rivers.

Recently, his travels have taken him to the jungle rivers of Central America for tarpon and snook, as well as to the fabled Atlantic salmon rivers of the USSR's Kola Peninsula. George selects Atlantic salmon (both freshwater and sea-run), steelhead, coho salmon, tarpon and sailfish as his favorite gamefish.

Between fishing adventures, George sits at a typewriter and transposes his experiences onto paper; he has worked as a full-time outdoor writer for 25 years.

Among other writing projects, George has written a

twice-weekly column in *The (Montreal) Gazette* for the past two decades. He is also a regular contributor to the *Atlantic Salmon Journal* and writes articles for various other outdoor-oriented publications. George also has written and produced *Gruenefeld's Atlantic Salmon River Log - Gaspé Region*, a guide which salmon anglers consider indispensable for anyone who fishes the salmon rivers of Quebec's Gaspé Peninsula.

George resides in Montreal, Quebec, Canada, with his favorite fishing companion, Debbie.

Bill Hilts Jr., born in the community of Niagara Falls, New York in 1956, has lived in the western New York area most of his life. Living between the Great Lakes of Erie and Ontario has had its advantages from a sportfishing point of view.

Bill has enjoyed the great outdoors with his family and friends since he was a boy. His grandfather, Irvin V. Hilts, ran a successful fishing camp in northern Ontario for many years. Irvin then traveled around the North American continent camping and fishing with his wife Dorothy. (Frequently, Bill Jr. would tag along.)

Bill's father, Bill Hilts Sr., a well-known outdoor writer, sparked Bill's interest in the outdoors and the desire to write about it.

Bill's mother, Sylvia, continues to be a tremendous influence, as are his brothers Rick and Dave, and sister Susan.

Bill now writes the *Niagara Falls Gazette* column that his dad wrote for many years. He also is an associate or field editor for the *New York State Conservation Council Comments, New York Sportsman* magazine, *Walleye* magazine and *ESLO Gazette.* He has also had a number of articles published in other outdoor publications.

Bill gets involved when it comes to the Great Lakes as a natural resource. Since his graduation from the State University of New York at Oswego—on Lake Ontario—with a bachelor's degree in communications, Bill has been active with numerous upstate New York sportfishing and conservation organizations, as well as serving on various committees with the New York State Conservation Council. He is also active in several outdoor writing organizations, and has won several awards for his writing.

Since 1986, he has worked full-time with the Niagara County Tourism offices in New York promoting fishing. It's an ideal job for a dedicated sportsman and conservationist who grew up on these Great Lakes, enjoying and preserving this splendid resource. Bill has convinced his bosses that he needs to be out on the water, fishing and catching fish, in order to provide first-hand information to the general public. So, each year he manages to wet a line about 100 to 125 days.

Milt Keizer was born in northwestern Sioux County, Iowa, more than half a century ago. When he was seven or eight, Milt discovered the town of Hawarden's Dry Creek wasn't so "dry." It, and gravel pits near the town's edge, held jillions of bluegill, sunfish, carp, bullhead and bass. When Milt was 10, a birthday bicycle freed him to roam the banks of the Big Sioux River in pursuit of catfish, buffalo, sheephead and walleye.

As a teenager, Milt fished Iowa, South Dakota and Minnesota waters, capping high school graduation with a four-day angling trip to Lake of the Woods (on the Minnesota-

Canadian border) for smallmouth bass, walleye, pike and muskellunge.

Milt served three years with the U.S. Marine Corps, seeing Korean conflict action, being wounded, and then returning to the U.S. to begin three years of journalism studies at the University of Iowa. Between his third and final years of college, he spent 12 years with a shovel and crane manufacturer, the last five in Ontario, Canada, where stream fishing yielded satisfying bass, trout and pike action. He also participated in "the good years" of bassing on the north side of Lake Erie. The opening of walleye and pike fishing in the northern half of the province is one of the rites of spring that he definitely enjoyed.

In 1967, Milt returned to the University of Iowa to complete his bachelor's degree in journalism. The next summer, he, wife Joelle and four young children, with a 10- by 12-foot tent and a small boat, camped and fished westward across the country for three months until they reached Washington state. There, Milt encountered, and became enthralled with steelhead, trout and salmon fishing.

Milt has been an editor for a weekly outdoor newspaper. He also co-founded a regional fishing magazine and edited it for eight years. He now is a freelance outdoor writer, as well as author and editor of several fishing books and a hunting education manual.

Milt would rather fish for salmonids now than for anything else that swims. He says the Pacific Ocean's transformation of 6-inch smolts into yard-long explosions of silver fury and awesome power never ceases to amaze him. Milt concludes, "Every hookup is a quality experience; every day, every hour I can fish is one of thankful appreciation."

Foreword

N orth American Fishing Club members who have had the privilege of catching one or more of the various species of salmon undoubtedly will never forget their first encounter with these regal fish. And, why should they? Salmon have captured anglers' hearts for centuries. Ask a salmon lover why and you'll get dozens of reasons. Well-known writer and NAFC friend Jim Bashline doesn't even try. In his book *Atlantic Salmon Fishing* he writes simply: "Yes, sensuous; I'm in love with the Atlantic salmon."

If you wanted to, you could divide the salmon of North America into two categories: Atlantic and Pacific, with all but one of the species falling into the latter. Just as easily you could break salmon fishing in North America down into three fisheries, the West Coast, the Great Lakes and the rivers along the East Coast (though the Dakotas, Idaho and New Mexico may holler). And, that is what we have done here.

Salmon Coast To Coast is unlike any other salmon book ever written because it truly covers salmon fishing coast to coast. Other salmon books generally focus on one species or one fishery, but we cover all inland and landlocked species *and* the three major North American fisheries.

It gives you a close-up look at salmon and their amazing anadromous life cycles, explaining theories on how these incredible animals evolved. More importantly, it provides everything in the way of knowledge and equipment you'll need to catch these beautiful, hard-fighting fish.

What sort of rod best handles the strain of being bent double when fishing with downriggers and still has enough muscle to bulldog a big chinook to the boat? How about the tackle you'll need if you're going to fish Pacific Coast rivers? What sort of fly fishing gear do hardcore Atlantic salmon anglers use? *Salmon Coast To Coast* reveals all, including insights on choosing the ideal trolling or drift boat.

When it comes to baits, lures and flies for enticing big salmon, you'll find this book to be one of your best sources of information. Likewise, we've compiled more than 60 pages that are devoted to various fishing techniques. It outlines, in no-nonsense terms, the popular as well as the lesser-known methods for catching big fish.

To complete the arduous task, we enlisted the help of three well-known outdoor writers, each of whom specializes in the salmon fishing found in their area. Montreal, Quebec, native George Gruenefeld, for example, has been fishing Atlantic salmon for decades and has written numerous articles on this wonderful fish.

Great Lakes salmon enthusiasts will probably find the name Bill Hilts Jr. familiar. Bill has lived in western New York for most of his life and has written numerous articles about the incredible salmon fishing in the Great Lakes, particularly in Lake Ontario.

Milt Keizer, an Iowa native now living in the Northwest, covers the amazingly diverse West Coast salmon fishery where the chinook salmon is king, but coho (silvers), sockeye, pinks and chum salmon fill the rest of the royal court.

Let's slow down for a minute. In fact, why don't you close your eyes and picture yourself fishing the best salmon waters in the world. What kind of tackle are you using? Are you in a boat and, if so, what kind? Finally, what species of salmon are you targeting?

I bet a number of you are casting flies or Pixie spoons into an Alaskan river—the Kenai, probably—full of kings and/or silvers. A certain percentage of you probably are in the backs of big Great Lakes boats trying to thread a huge, feisty king around downrigger cables and into a stout landing net. And, no doubt, many of you picture yourself in Quebec's wild Gaspé Peninsula battling a 20-pound Atlantic that spends more time in the air than in the water.

There are the many other fantastic salmon locations across this great land that you could be fishing.

That's the thing about salmon and salmon fishing—there is something for everyone. Salmon are no longer a fish for kings alone. Indeed, there once was a day when men died for "poaching" the king's salmon. Today, however, through extensive stocking and careful fishery management, salmon are now available in numerous waters in many states and provinces. In fact, good salmon fishing is only a few hours air-time away from the majority of you who are reading this. True, stocks are depleted in some areas, but outstanding fishing—salmon fishing—is still available.

I hope you enjoy *Salmon Coast To Coast!*

Steve Pennaz
Executive Director
North American Fishing Club

All About
Salmon

1

Great Lakes Salmon

Salmon On! It's not a cry that has just developed the last few years, especially within the history-rich Great Lakes Basin. The sport of angling has deep roots throughout the region; early documented accounts cover three centuries. And, the fish species that has long commanded the most attention has been the salmon—the subject of this book.

"Earliest accounts of fishing in the Great Lakes Basin that we've been able to determine in our research—which, of course, would be associated with the (American) Indian—date back to 1678," said David Urso, head of the Sportfishing Resource Center that is being put together as an important part of the Aquarium of Niagara Falls, New York.

The 1678 documentation results from French priest Father Hennepin's travels into the Niagara Frontier with General LaSalle. Hennepin wrote of how, for the local Seneca and Missisauga Indians, the fishery was an important mainstay of their diet. They used nets weighted with rocks in favorite pools and eddies in the lower Niagara River where fish were known to frequent, with whitefish being the primary targeted species.

"Hennepin also writes of Indians catching brook trout by quickly snatching fish up by hand," said Urso, who is an avid angler. "Wire traps were also used as a method for taking fish on the Niagara River.

"Hennepin's writing also indicated that an 86-pound trout was caught while he was here, but this fish was believed to be a

This 30-pound, 12-ounce coho salmon held the record for cohos caught in the Great Lakes from 1985 to 1989. It was displaced by a 33-pound, 4-ounce monster. Both were taken from the Salmon River, a Lake Ontario tributary, in upstate New York.

Great Lakes Salmon   15

Niagara River sturgeon or large Atlantic salmon mistaken for a trout."

Early settlers learned quickly from the Indian, and it wasn't long before spears, nets, traps and hook or line were all put into use for taking fish on a regular basis. Fish continued to be an important food supplement for the Indian until the mid-19th century.

It's recorded that in the mid-1800s, Seneca Indians from the Tonawanda Reservation (some 40 miles from the Lake Ontario shoreline) made annual trips to the lake to catch a year's supply of fish. Women were sent a day in advance to the mouths of Fish, Eighteen Mile and Golden Hill creeks to set up camp, with the men arriving the following day with spears, nets and hooks in hand. After a year's supply of fish was caught, the women cleaned, smoked and dried the fish.

It was about this same time that the fishing resource seemed to be affected. Fish numbers seemed to dwindle throughout most of the Great Lakes, especially Lake Ontario. As a result, the Niagara River Anglers Club was formed in 1886. The club's objectives included passing laws that would prohibit use of nets and dynamite as viable methods for taking fish in the Niagara River, Lake Ontario tributaries and the Erie Canal. The Niagara River Anglers Club also initiated an extensive stocking program for various fish species.

Through these efforts and the work of conservation officer Daniel Pomeroy during the early 1900s, fish populations rebounded. But, commercial fishing, intense fishing pressure, and—later—pollution, all contributed to the demise of certain fisheries. Lake Ontario, for example, which had a worldwide reputation for its Atlantic salmon fishery, saw its popular fish species slowly die out.

Because of intense fishing pressure, heavy industrial development and the resulting pollution, many important pieces of the Great Lakes fishery have been lost forever. Blue pike are now considered an extinct species. Sturgeon are on the endangered list. Atlantic salmon disappeared. These things are irreplaceable. The few concerned sportsmen of yesteryear weren't enough to make a lasting impact.

In the 1960s, the Great Lakes were given a second chance of again being a viable fishery. Through the efforts of a number

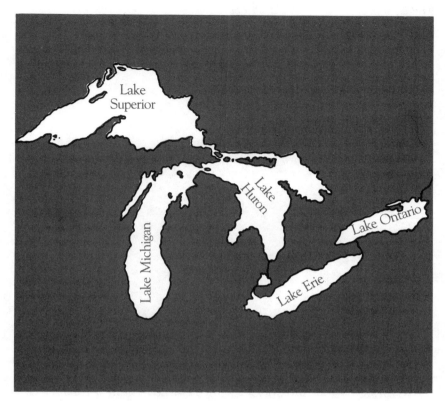

The five water bodies making up the Great Lakes represent the largest, contiguous freshwater body in the world. These lakes also represent some of the world's best fishing, especially since Pacific salmon were introduced in 1966. Lakes Superior, Michigan and Huron are referred to as the upper Great Lakes.

of people, the Great Lakes have experienced a sportfishing rebirth that is second to none. The Great Lakes—Superior, Michigan, Huron, Erie and Ontario—combine to contain more than one-third of all the freshwater in the world. And, with revitalization of sportfishing, the lakes offer both quality and quantity fishing.

Lake Michigan was the first to be stocked with Pacific salmon when Michigan's Department of Natural Resources introduced coho salmon in three streams in 1966. The following year, the first stocking of chinook salmon took place, with the first open-water fishery for cohos that same year. With the early success in Lake Michigan documented, similar stocking programs followed in the other Great Lakes. Salmon undoubtedly were the headline act.

Chinook Salmon

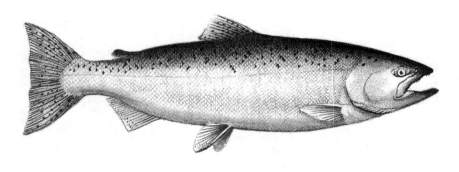

Chinook salmon, often called kings, have silvery sides with small dark spots on the back and both tail lobes. The chinook's teeth are set in black gums, and the lower jaw comes to a sharp point. Other common names include spring salmon, tyee, quinnat, blackmouth and blackjaw.

Species Availability

Chinook or king salmon (*Oncohynchus tshawytscha*) is the true "king" of the Great Lakes Basin. The chinook sports an elongated body with its color ranging from dark green to grey, fading to silvery sides, and light silver to white on its belly. It has black spots on its back, dorsal fin and tail. When spawning, the male chinook turns almost black while the female remains slightly lighter in color. Chinooks have relatively small eyes and a distinct, dark lateral line running from the back of the eye to the tail. A quick identification feature is the chinook's black mouth with dark gums.

Experimental stockings of triploid chinook salmon by the state of Michigan have taken place in Lake Michigan as part of a 5-year pilot project. In theory, salmon eggs are treated at 83.5 degrees (Fahrenheit) for 10 minutes. Although there's only about 17 percent survival, the remaining eggs that make it through the process become sterile, with the resulting fish losing their desire to spawn. It is believed that these fish, without that instinctive desire driving them into the tributary streams, could live to be eight or nine years old and achieve

Complete Angler's Library

Coho Salmon

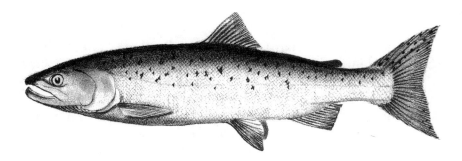

The coho salmon, also known as silver salmon or blueback, has small black spots on its sides and back, as does the chinook, but only on the upper tail lobe. It has silvery sides with bluish or greenish coloration on the back. While its lower jaw is blunter than the chinooks, a quick identification is that the coho's teeth are set in whitish to grayish gums.

sizes of more than 50 pounds—if they survive that long. Early reports have shown that these fish, in the early years, have been highly susceptible to sportfishing methods. As a result, only a very small percentage make it past five years of age.

When Michigan discontinued its triploid program in 1991, New York state started a similar program, with stocking occurring that spring. Officials acknowledged it would take time to determine the success of the triploid fish experiment. Meanwhile, the mature standard diploid Pacific salmon, be it chinook or coho, will die after its mandatory fall spawning run.

Coho Salmon

Coho salmon, a cousin of the chinook, and also a Pacific salmon, has a torpedo-shaped body. Average size ranges from 5 to 15 pounds, although a world-record, all-tackle catch weighing 33 pounds, 4 ounces came from the Salmon River, a Lake Ontario tributary, in 1989.

The coho's back is olive green to steel blue and black, with black spots on its back and upper tail lobe. The sides are silver in color with fine scales, and the belly is light-colored. The coho has 13 to 15 anal fin rays and a black mouth with whitish gums.

Although the coho is less powerful than the king, it's a popular species noted for twisting, acrobatic bouts with anglers.

Atlantic Salmon

The Atlantic Salmon is one of two salmonid species indigenous to the Lake Ontario portion of the Great Lakes Basin. Atlantics have been unable to migrate any further into the Great Lakes because of the Niagara Falls.

Atlantic salmon, which are often confused with brown trout, do not die after spawning as do Pacific salmon. Atlantics were extremely sensitive to changes in Lake Ontario that adversely affected the species, so the last report of an Atlantic indigenous to the Great Lakes being caught was in 1898.

However, with the accelerated basin cleanup, and the success of other salmon stocking programs in the Great Lakes, several states including New York and Michigan, as well as Canada's Ontario province, have initiated Atlantic salmon stocking programs.

Atlantic salmon are olive brown to green on the dorsal surface, with the sides and belly silver in color. They usually carry X-shaped markings on the side and back, and the tail is deeply forked. Atlantics are noted for their spectacular fighting and leaping ability when caught.

Pink Salmon

These fish were first introduced in Lake Superior around Thunder Bay and the Current River in 1956. Mature adults arose three years later. By 1971, pink salmon had become widespread. They were documented to be in Lake Huron in 1969, and Lake Michigan in 1973. By 1979, they appeared in Lakes Erie and Ontario.

In Lake Superior, the pink salmon usually spawns during odd-numbered years, although there have been numerous exceptions reported of 3-year-old fish spawning during even-number years.

Returning adults' average size is 17 to 19 inches in length and about 4 pounds in weight. Coloration varies from bluish to greenish along the dorsal, shading to silver on the sides and white in the ventral region. The back, upper sides and both tail lobes have large, round or oval spots.

Lake Ontario

In surface area, Lake Ontario is the smallest of the Great Lakes. However, it is the third deepest and probably the best suited, as far as forage populations go, for salmonid stockings. Early-season action for chinook and coho salmon traditionally concentrates in Ontario's Western Basin, with the primary focus being the mighty Niagara River—the single biggest source of water flowing into the lake.

At the mouth of this powerful river is the Niagara Bar, one of the finest, springtime freshwater "hotspots" in the world. Three types of structure—bottom, thermal and current—requirements can be found here, attracting millions of forage fish, as well as prey fish.

The Niagara Bar is by no means small, but fishing activity doesn't need to be restricted to the bar itself. The waters toward St. Catherines, Ontario, as well as the U.S. ports of Wilson, Olcott and Oak Orchard/Point Breeze (on through to Rochester) all help make this popular Western Basin what it is. Some salmon can be caught further east, but for most consistent catches, target the west.

During early-season action, one of the best tips for a beginner is to stay away from the pack. With fish closer to the surface and in shallower water, they'll spook much easier under extreme fishing pressure. Staying away from other boats should help improve your success ratio. As Ontario's water warms, fish will scatter throughout the lake.

During the summer months, however, the northern shore of Lake Ontario is very good for deep water trolling. Fish will also be dispersed to the east, off such popular ports as Sodus Bay, Fairhaven, Port Ontario and Henderson Harbor. Bigger concentrations of fish will take place in August and September as migrating salmon make their way back to stocking sites, especially to the Salmon River, home of New York's ultramodern fish hatchery. This is where all of New York's salmon and trout stockings come from for Lakes Erie and Ontario.

Lake Erie

Lake Erie is the shallowest of all the Great Lakes. This is

normally not conducive to good fishing. Coho is probably the No. 1 quarry for anglers in Erie, utilizing small boats close to shore off nearly every one of the tributary streams from New York to Ohio to cash-in on some super salmon and trout action. From the first thaw in March until May, anglers often welcome a change of pace from the walleye and bass fishing.

Fishing the tributary mouths should get you in the right frame of mind while trolling. Target New York and Pennsylvania shorelines. In Pennsylvania, most salmon anglers tackle the Presque Isle Bay area. The coho is the primary target, but a few kings will be encountered.

If you're looking for other salmon concentrations, head to the westernmost waters of Erie, off the shores of Michigan and Ontario. Early-season action can be found there, too. As the waters warm, concentrate on the deeper Eastern Basin. Excellent fall runs occur off Pennsylvania's and New York's shores.

Summer salmon receives little pressure. It's not until August that staging kings and cohos receive attention from boaters, and into September for tributary fishermen.

Lake Huron

This is one lake that doesn't receive as much publicity as it should. It's not an easy lake to fish, but the rewards are there. Early in the year, the southern portion of the lake is usually the hottest area for fishing. Warm water discharges on the St. Clair River attract both salmon and trout in search of food.

Temperature is a key for finding fish, because there is little structure underneath the surface. Fish have a tendency to move a lot, going where wind and water currents dictate.

Of this list, the chinook is the No. 1 species to target, migrating up and down the coast as the season progresses.

At Port Huron, current is a factor near the river. Canadian waters can hold good fish, depending on weather conditions. Baitfish, and the presence of temperature breaks will both be keys for success. Most of the bigger kings will be taken close to shore during the early season.

By July 1, salmon will start moving to deeper waters, into the 60- to 120-foot range. Come fall, springtime conditions will once again occur, so the same areas will be fished.

This salmon is evidence that sea lampreys are a serious problem in the Great Lakes Basin. Possible cutbacks in control funding don't alleviate fishermen's fears, either. Lamprey control is handled by the Great Lakes Fisheries Commission.

Lake Michigan

Lake Michigan also holds true for your standard formula for early angling options—head to the south. Both Michigan City and Gary, Indiana, are targeted areas that should produce well for you, primarily due to the quicker warming trends attracting the baitfish. Ditto for St. Joseph's, Michigan—primarily for cohos. It's in the south where you'll often find ample numbers of chinook and coho salmon, and quite a few trout.

Moving north along the Michigan shoreline, salmon action normally diminishes in the spring. However, the weather plays an important role throughout the winter as to how good the fishing will be in the spring. If a mild winter occurs, coho salmon might not have a tendency to make the long trip south. Hence, better fishing at ports such as Ludington and Manistee.

Wisconsin anglers have a good inshore fishery on their side of the lake in the spring, trolling or casting near Milwaukee, Racine, Kenosha and Sheboygan. Coho fishing can be spectacular in the southern portions of Wisconsin, with those waters warming quickest and attracting baitfish. The best chinook fishing in the spring takes place off Washington Island along the "thumb." Green Bay can do well on salmonids, as well. Move north as the season progresses if you're looking for active salmon, although pockets of fish can be found along the entire Wisconsin coast throughout the year.

Wisconsin fishermen, in fact, have a geographical advantage when it comes to cold-water fish species, especially in summer when waters turn warm. Prevailing westerly winds blow warmer waters to the east, bringing in colder water—and plenty of fish.

Lake Superior

Steelhead and lake trout are the two top salmonid species receiving the most attention from Lake Superior anglers. However, there certainly is good coho and chinook salmon fishing, too. Some Atlantic salmon are found, but the overall program hasn't been too successful.

Off the shores of the Upper Peninsula of Michigan, salmon fishing is usually available closer to shore. Jim Maki, a charter skipper out of Marquette, Michigan, specializes in salmon during both the spring and the fall. His fishing will start up toward the end of April and will continue into the first week of June. In the spring, the waters of Superior are still cold, so any slight advantage to temperature is a key to pinpointing fish. Shallower areas close to shore, especially off creek and river mouths, will be likely locations for slightly warmer temperatures. These will also be areas that attract spawning baitfish, bringing in the salmon to feed.

Few fish are actually stocked in Superior's salmon fishery. One of the saving graces is the natural reproduction that is helping to supplement salmon numbers. Michigan stocks coho and chinook, but Wisconsin only stocks about 400,000 chinook and no cohos. Despite low numbers, Wisconsin enjoys some good salmon fishing, especially for coho, along the shoreline, throughout the Apostle Islands and into Duluth and Superior.

Fishing along the Minnesota shoreline, up to Thunder Bay, is better in the summer when the waters warm.

For the most part, salmon are tough to target in the summer months due to the lake's size. They become more of an incidental catch until they start showing up in the areas they stocked or grew up in. Salmon fanciers will target the middle of August to tackle mature salmon—at least, for kings. The cohos come in a bit later, toward the end of August or the first week in September. They'll also stay later, into October.

Other Inland Salmon Programs

Many other salmon stocking programs have been initiated around the country, with mixed results. Here is a look at a few of those programs in several states between the two coasts, and outside the Great Lakes Basin, where good conditions exist for establishing salmon.

Idaho

Although this popular Western state already gets some native fish running the rivers, the state's fish and game department has gotten involved with some inland stockings of salmon. The lake with the most noteworthy reputation continues to be Coeur d'Alene.

Since 1982, when stocking started with a Bonneville strain, the state has been planting anywhere from 10,000 to 60,000 chinook salmon. A Lake Michigan strain has taken over, and most recently, those annual numbers have settled in on 40,000. In addition to the stocking efforts, fisheries experts believe they're getting another 40,000 fish from natural reproduction.

Kokanee salmon are also made available through stocking efforts that kicked off in the 1950s. Natural reproduction has since taken over for the kokanee, with fish 1 to 6 inches—a good forage for the chinook salmon. Nine to 10-inch fish offer great catch options for anglers looking for easy action, and they are very good eating. Estimated population in the lake is 10 million kokanee.

The early stage of the chinook program produced the state record catch, a 42-pounder. Since the mid-1980s, though, 30-pound-class kings are produced on occasion.

According to Idaho fisheries biologist Melo Maiolie, the winter period from December to February offers excellent catch rate options in 70 to 130 feet of water. August is also a very good time, because it is the period when fish enter the pre-spawn mode.

North Dakota

The main body of water receiving salmon stockings is Lake

Bill Pearce, considered the father of New York state's salmonid stocking program, takes time out to catch a nice king salmon. For his work as an employee in establishing the stocking of Lakes Erie and Ontario, the New York State Department of Environmental Conservation named its principal Great Lakes salmon and trout plants hatchery at Altmar on the Salmon River for Pearce.

Sakakawea, northwest of Bismarck. It's one of the largest reservoirs on the Missouri River system. Salmon were introduced to this major waterway in 1971 when North Dakota's game and fish department kicked off a coho salmon stocking program which included the first stockings of rainbow smelt.

After 10 years, however, the stocking of coho ended because of a lack of results. In 1976, the state added chinook stockings, and the results have been much better. Lake trout were stocked from 1973 to 1984, and steelhead throughout the 1980s. Most recently, brown trout have been added to Lake Sakakawea's stocking inventory.

In Sakakawea, July-August is the most popular time for fishing salmon, with the Garrison Dam area the most popular spot on the lake. West Coast tactics seem to outperform Great Lakes fishing techniques. Anglers use live bait rigs incorporating anchovy or herring strips, as well as dodgers and flashers. Downriggers are also used. The state record fish, a 31-pound, 2-ounce chinook taken in the Garrison Dam tailrace, was caught in 1986. This fish either came up the Missouri River system from South Dakota, or it was a lucky king that made it through the dam. The North Dakota coho record is 10 pounds, 2 ounces.

South Dakota

Salmon stockings in South Dakota lakes, launched in 1982 by the state's department of game, fish and parks with a stocking of about 100,000 chinook, are restricted to Missouri River reservoirs. Lake Oahe, the primary location for inland kings, has a water stretch of 230 miles, extending into neighboring North Dakota.

Smelt imitations are the No. 1 enticement, copying the primary forage for these popular fish. Early spring, and late summer-early fall are the top calendar targets for salmon trollers, especially along the face of the Oahe Dam and north from Spring Creek to the Cheyenne River. The state record is 20 pounds, 3 ounces. In 1990, Oahe received 66,000 fish.

New Mexico

Although New Mexico is not often considered a water-rich state, three man-made reservoirs within its boundaries have received landlocked kokanee salmon stockings, said Steve Henry, chief of fisheries management.

Heron Lake has been stocked since the mid-1970s. Each year, the lake receives 400,000 to 500,000, 2-inch fingerlings. Four-year-old fish will range in size from 14 to 17 inches long, with 15-inch fish being an average for mature salmon. Trolling boats work the lake from April to November, with shore fishing taking place during December and January.

Navajo Reservoir is a large impoundment formed from several rivers in the northwest corner of the state, near the Colorado border. Both states stock the reservoir—having done so since the mid-1970s—with about 400,000 to 500,000 fish annually. El Vado Reservoir near Heron Lake in north-central New Mexico receives about 200,000, 2-inch fingerlings annually.

2

West Coast Salmon

hen the first waves of American settlers arrived in what is now Oregon and Washington in the late 1700s to mid-1800s, there were uncountable millions of salmon. On annual spawning runs, huge, silver fish choked most northern coastal rivers with the press of their bodies. Many salmon plugged the rivers; no one could imagine an ending, ever, to their prolific numbers.

Dried and smoked salmon were traded by Indians to white pioneers for more than a century. In 1937, area residents bartered for salmon with Washington's Chehalis tribe.

Trailblazers Merriwether Lewis and George Rogers Clark often mentioned the salmon and "little salmon"—now known to be steelhead—they encountered and fished while forging down the Columbia River to reach the Pacific Ocean. Although their party's angling was undoubtedly for sustenance, Captain Lewis's journal may be the first written record of West Coast salmon angling.

By the turn of the 20th century, hundreds of salmon canneries were each shipping thousands of tons of tinned salmon to East Coast and European markets. Alaska was acknowledged as the leading early salmon-canning area by virtue of its 1920-1930 annual average pack of about 300 million pounds.

Sportfishermen also began to appear along river banks and on bays and sounds in the early 20th century. The Alaska

A 1¾-ounce Krocodile Flutter Jig did the job for this angler as she hauled in a 35-pound chinook beauty, while fishing with well-known angler Buzz Ramsey. In this case, fishing during the fall run paid off handsomely as the angler used tactics outlined in this book.

West Coast Salmon 29

Game Commission's head at that time—Frank Dufresne—was also a devoted angler and author. He wrote books and articles for several outdoor magazines. He often advocated taking salmon with spinners, lures and, later, Pacific salmon flies.

Renowned writers and fishermen Zane Grey, Roderick Haig-Brown and Joe Brooks also extolled the halcyon days of salmon fishing on West Coast waters in articles written from the mid-1920s into the 1950s.

Threats To Salmon Runs

Logging, farming, town and city growth, home-building and dam construction with the resultant siltation, pollution and reduced water flow in many rivers cut so drastically into a number of fish populations that some salmon "strains" peculiar to specific rivers or watersheds are now extinct or endangered. Other salmon "runs" are now sustained largely because of restocking efforts by fisheries management departments.

However, enough strong runs of wild-spawned salmon in Alaska and British Columbia, particularly, and the hatchery-enhanced, still-existent stocks along America's West Coast permit a very viable, popular and productive salmon sportfishery today.

It is a vital source of income for the Pacific Coast economy. Multiply licenses sold by lodging, travel, bait, boat, repairs, fuel, tackle and lures, food and accessories costs and you will get a high, multi-million-dollar figure.

In 1989, for example, nearly 1.4 million salmon sportfishing licenses were sold in the northern coastal states and Canada's British Columbia province, and nearly 3.8 million fish were harvested. California doesn't maintain statistics on salmon but estimates nearly 250,000 salmon were taken in that state in 1989. (In California, the state's general fishing permit includes the taking of salmon, so no special permit is required.)

Salmon Ancestry/Identification

All salmon, trout and char are believed to be descended from a common Pleistocene Age progenitor. This "family tree" branched toward a discriminatory difference in which Pacific salmon all die after spawning. Atlantic salmon, anadromous trout and char do not necessarily die after undergoing out-migration, traumas of chemical and body changes from fresh- to saltwater and salt- to freshwater and the rigors of spawning. A high ratio of attrition occurs among Atlantic salmon, steelhead and sea-going cutthroat and brown trout.

Many Western salmon and their relatives look very much alike in saltwater, and when first entering spawning streams. West Coast fishermen have adopted a quick and literal "rule of thumb" to distinguish among chinook, coho salmon and large steelhead, which are the nearest look-alike and most commonly confused heavyweights of the salmonid species. By carefully gripping a fish's lower jaw tip between thumb and forefinger and prying open the mouth, anglers can quickly check the coloration of the jaw line and the mouth's lining. (See description in Chapter 1.)

Sportfishermen's Targets

Five Pacific salmon species furnish inshore sport angling along the Pacific coastline from mid-California to northern Alaskan waters. These are chinook (*Oncorhynchus tshawytscha*), chum (*Onchorhynchus keta*), coho (*Onchorhynchus kisutch*), sockeye (*Onchorhynchus nerka*) and pink (*Onchorhynchus gorbuscha*) salmon. A sixth Pacific salmon (*Onchorhynchus masou*), the Japanese cherry salmon, sometimes is netted off the Aleutian Islands, but very rarely is taken inland by sport-fishermen. Popular, productive off-coast sport salmon fisheries also exist along the entire Pacific seaboard, mid-California to Alaska.

Inshore fishing for West Coast salmon species takes place in sounds, straits, lagoons, bays, estuaries, inlets and rivers, as well as in some lakes and reservoirs stocked by California, Oregon, Idaho, Washington, and the province of British Columbia.

Chinook Salmon

The largest and most-sought of the Pacific salmon fivesome is the chinook salmon, also known as king, blackmouth, tule, spring and Tyee. The name, "King," derives from the chinook's size, largest of the West Coast salmon. "Blackmouth" is the name applied to feeding salmon ranging in size from a few pounds to 30 pounds which chose not to migrate from bays, sounds or straits into the Pacific.

Blackmouth salmon also originate as hatchery stocks deliberately released late in order to maintain a resident fishery in nearby waters. "Tule" is a quick-to-darken late summer or fall fish such as those that return in July and August to the Columbia River. Canadian anglers fish for local, inshore "springs" in May, June and July. "Tyee" (Indian name for chief) is the respectful title applied to late summer and fall British Columbia chinook weighing more than 30 pounds.

World Record

Anglers attempting to take a record chinook know escalation of the record awaits only time, place, fish and angler. Chinook far larger than current records have appeared in commercial net catches, as indicated by the wall mount of a 126-pound, 2-ounce netted Alaskan fish—nearly 30 pounds over the rod-and-reel record of the time—displayed through the 1970s and early 1980s by a Seattle taxidermy firm. In 1989, a 105-pound chinook reportedly was netted from the Skeena River (B.C.) in an Indian fishery.

Sport catches of West Coast chinook generally average 15 to 35 pounds, with larger specimens highlighting each season and particular rivers in each state and British Columbia regularly producing 50- and 60-pound fish.

Freshly arrived from maturation in the Pacific Ocean, "mint" condition chinook salmon are cream white on the belly, have gleaming silver sides, and their black-spotted backs will be any shade of glistening chrome green, brilliant bronze, metallic blue or mirror gray. Chinook prefer large streams or smaller watercourses having deep holes and runs for reproduction. They travel hundreds to more than 1,000 miles on spawning trips up rivers free of dams or high falls.

Soon after entering spawning streams, male chinook undergo a change from gleaming saltwater colors to rust-red or dirty-black backs, mottled, gray sides and yellowing paunches. A pronounced hook, called a kype, develops at the male salmon's jaw tip, in which long, sharp teeth stud black gumlines within a gray-fleshed mouth.

The females of the chinook species often retain their beauty for hundreds of river miles and many weeks longer than males, fading slowly into silver-gray or bronze backs, peach and tan

While there may be some difficulty identifying different salmon species, an angler would have no trouble with this "mint condition," fall chinook taken in Oregon's Alsea River. This is as shiny as ocean fish arrive back in their natal streams.

sides and often showing a blush of rose or scarlet on cheeks and gill plates. By the end of spawning, a female salmon's forked tail is often as worn as a well-used broom from sweeping gravel. Her nose will become scratched and raw from thrusting into the gravel to dig her "redd" before depositing eggs.

Where the protective mucous coating of salmon is scraped or rubbed off, fungus infection may rapidly set in and the salmon then appears to have patches of fuzz on its head or body. This growth resembles the "flock" coating of automobile dashes popular in the 1950s. The fungus speeds deterioration of the salmon's flesh, ruining it for tablefare.

Chinook Life Cycle

Chinook salmon generally spawn in August to November,

although "seasonal runs" of fish approach their gravel redds at varying times of spring, summer and fall. Like all salmon, they have extremely efficient and selective olfactory senses and can trace a few parts per million of the chemical effluents leading them to their birth streams to lay eggs. It's often within yards of the same spot where they as alevins first emerged from their own eggs to feed, absorb sustaining yolk sacs and become fry.

Next, as fingerlings, young salmon avidly feed and grow rapidly into the parr stage, when large, dark, mottled spots cover their broadening backs. As smolts of 5 to 9 inches, they are ready to move downriver to the ocean and their colors have changed again to shimmering platinum sides, white bellies and bold, dark backs with distinct spots.

A precocious chinook "jack" salmon may barely sniff saltwater before returning at one or two years of age, sufficiently sexually mature to aid in the spawning effort. Most chinook, however, spend three to four years at sea. Heavy eaters that ignore spawning urges until their sixth or seventh year become the giants of their clan.

Coho Salmon

Coho salmon are the second most important sportfish of the West Coast salmon species and share with chinook the greatest popularity with Western salmon anglers. Also called "silver salmon" and "hooknose," coho are aggressive biters and acrobatic leapers that average around 8 pounds, but grow to a world-record size of 31 pounds. Some rivers have strains of large coho salmon consistently weighing near 20 pounds.

Coho salmon ocean colors are bright, green-blue backs speckled with black dots, flashing silver sides and oyster-shell white stomachs. There are no spots on the lower half of a coho's caudal fin (tail). Male coho that linger in saltwater until late September or longer before returning to their natal streams develop a feature that early-arriving males also acquire later, pronounced "kypes" to both upper and lower jaw tips (sometimes the jaw tips overlap), thus earning them the "hooknose" name.

After entering freshwater, a male coho rapidly undergoes a color change to rust and gray coloration, and the female shows rose and black tinges on gills while her svelte flanks gradually fade to mousy, mottled gray.

Coho range from mid-Californian to Alaskan waters but feed much closer to their native shorelines than do chinook salmon. Most coho migrate in the spring to the Pacific Ocean for one or two years, with a few 3-salt-year strains. They pursue baitfish near the surface, betraying their location by leaping and splashing when feeding on a school of hapless herring. These eating binges also are often marked by gulls joining in the attack.

Silver salmon returning from the Pacific Ocean often continue to gorge on available baitfish—herring, candlefish and anchovies—after entering straits, sounds, inlets, estuaries and bays. Many fish still retain this feeding instinct far upriver in spawning streams, even though their digestive tracts have shrunk to where they can make little use of food.

Coho salmon, very active fish, seem especially exuberant about entering freshwater. Their habit of leaping, rolling and "boiling" on the surface of rivers may be to loosen eggs and milt for spawning, or possibly to shake free of sea lice that cling to them for three to five days in freshwater. Perhaps it is just exhilaration upon returning instinctively to dimly remembered surroundings. This trait often exposes the coho's presence to knowledgeable anglers who watch for these indicators during early mornings and late evenings.

Coho spawn from October to early December in smaller rivers. A tiny tributary that has arm-span-wide gravel pools is sufficient. Coho salmon, year after year, will leave rivulets via a culvert to swim and struggle through no more than 5-inch-deep water in a roadside ditch, only to flop and scramble 30 to 50 more feet up a scarcely-wet hillside to deposit eggs in the loose gravel of a pair of spring-fed, 4-foot-diameter, water pools that are about 10 inches deep.

Coho have keen eyesight and hearing, and will often speed from 50 and 60 feet away to strike at what appears to be food. Sometimes, a Strait of Juan de Fuca (Washington) or Strait of Georgia (British Columbia) angler will see coho racing each other toward a trolled surface lure. He sees dorsal fins slicing the water in screaming arcs that zero-in on his hook-laden coho fly, bucktail, streamer or spinner, followed by an anticipation-heightened smashing strike.

West Coast Salmon   35

Sockeye Salmon

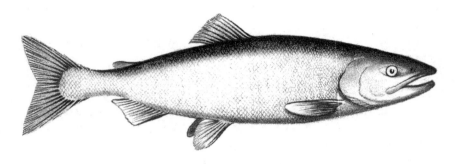

Sockeye salmon have no distinct black spots, although they may have black speckles on the back. Their sides are silvery with the back a brilliant steel-blue to bluish green coloring. They're also called red salmon, blueback salmon, and the landlocked species is often called kokanee, koke, redfish and silver trout.

Sockeye Salmon

Sockeye salmon, called "bluebacks" in some areas and "red salmon" in others, are small fish averaging 3 to 7 pounds. World-record size for sockeye, however, is over 16 pounds.

In saltwater, sockeye feed mostly on plankton and other minute ocean foods. In inshore areas, they once held a reputation as "the salmon that wouldn't bite." They range the Pacific from upper California to Alaska, but spawning seldom occurs in rivers below the Columbia. Most of these blue/gray-backed, burnished silver-sided and lightly-spotted salmon spawn from September to December in streams having lakes along their courses. The juvenile fish may stay from one to three years in the lakes, then head for saltwater for one to three years.

Non-migratory sockeye, called "kokanee" and "silver trout," spend their entire lives in freshwater and are delightful sport targets for anglers. Kokanee are an abundant, schooling fish that are eager biters, readily caught and good eating.

Upon entering freshwater, maturing sockeye males show very definite "shoulders" similar to, but smaller than, the humps of pink salmon, and they soon acquire typical salmonid

Pink Salmon

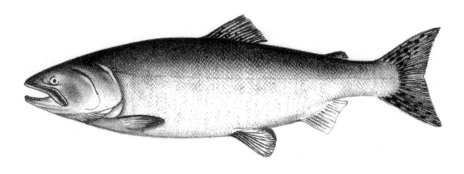

Pink salmon have characteristic silvery sides, and large black spots (some as large as the eye) on the upper sides, back and both tail lobes. Also known as the humpback salmon, spawning males develop a large hump in front of the dorsal fin, plus a kype and large canine teeth.

kypes on the tips of their jaws. Male sockeyes gradually turn dull brick-red. Females also undergo color changes on their sides and bellies to a splotchy, mustard-lime tone infused with carmine (a rich crimson).

The "non-biting" label applied to inshore sockeye tumbled, then died in the 1960s. On the Iliamna River, Alaska, anglers discovered sockeye strikes could be triggered. On the Kenai River, Alaskan fishermen also found sockeye would bite. Off Vancouver Island, salmon anglers sparked a sockeye fishery.

Perhaps the most successful sockeye fishing since the early 1970s has been on Lake Washington, a 23-mile-long lake pinched between Seattle and several eastside suburban cities. Fifteen-thousand to 25,000 sockeye bound for the Cedar River near the lake's south tip are caught in an average season. (See Chapter 20 for details on this special fishery.)

Pink Salmon

Although the smallest Pacific salmon species, pinks (also called humpbacked salmon and "humpies") generally are the most numerous in commercial catches and often eagerly sought

Chum Salmon

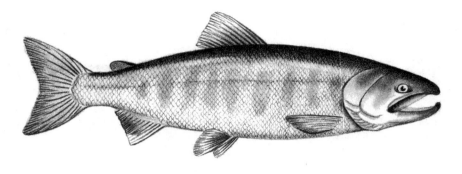

Silvery sides, often with faint vertical bands, distinguish chum salmon. These fish do not have dark spots, but their pupils are wider when compared to a sockeye. Other common names include dog salmon, calico salmon and autumn salmon.

by sport anglers. They're caught from California to Alaska.

The pink salmon's life cycle rarely exceeds two years. Fry migrate early from natal streams to saltwater, returning the following year in late spring and summer. Stream fisheries generally peak in August through September, prior to the November-December spawning period. Most pink salmon taken in sport catches range from 3 to 7 pounds.

Pink salmon have small scales, but larger spots in relation to body size than even their biggest chinook cousins. In saltwater, pinks have glossy blue-gray backs, polished chrome sides and cream white stomachs. However, in freshwater, the males' colors quickly fade and become mottled, and their backs, from immediately behind the head to rear of the dorsal fin, hump up like an American bison. Female pinks retain fat torpedo shapes in freshwater, but soon lose their salt-spangled brilliance. Their sides are vertical splotches of a brown-and-gray pattern.

Chum Salmon

Ocean-bright chum salmon have backs shading from pale green to bright blue, gleaming, small-scaled silver sides and shiny white stomachs. They are lightly speckled on back and tail with smaller spots than those of the chinook, which they closely resemble in saltwater.

Chum salmon's range extends from south of San Francisco to the Aleutian Islands. Spawning generally takes place in lower river stretches. Chum favor shallow riffles where side channels and tributaries enter main rivers for their daytime holding lies and will move to spawning redds in slightly deeper, slower water during periods of low-light levels.

In freshwater, both male and female chum salmon darken quickly to worn-out boot (brown) coloration on backs, and display purple or green vertical splotches on their sides with muddy-colored bellies. Male chum salmon also possess a fearsome display of teeth, similar to those of a wolf or dog, which explains the "dog salmon" name commonly given them, with typical kypes at tips of both jaws. Another nickname applied to chum salmon is "calico salmon" because of distinct vertical bands of color that show on their sides in freshwater.

Early, small "summer" chum salmon may appear in some natal streams during July to September, but major runs of large "fall chums" do not arrive until late September through November. Most chums weigh between 6 and 16 pounds. While the largest sport-caught chum salmon is in the 32-pound class, net-caught chums have been known to exceed 35 pounds.

Chums are best caught by trolling plugs or casting flashy nickel or brass-finish spinners and spoons having some red or orange spots, streaks or slashes. Drift-rig fishermen also trick them with cluster egg and shrimp baits or with green, lime or chartreuse, bobber-yarn combinations. Fifteen- to 20-pound chums are tough to handle on light tackle. Bull strong, they put up determined battles marked by long runs and stubborn surges, although smaller chums may plunge and roll on the surface.

3

Atlantic Coast Salmon

Before the birth of Christ, Emperor Julius Caesar's legions marched across western Europe. In the coastal rivers of the Western lands that they invaded, Roman soldiers came across a fish that moved like quicksilver up the cool, tumbling rivers. The Romans named this fish Salar—The Leaper.

Since Caesar's day, generation upon generation of men have been fascinated with these fish and, because of this curiosity, we pushed Atlantic salmon almost to the edge of extinction and back again. When studying the travels of Atlantic salmon in the freshwater rivers and in the open seas, we learned that they migrate from the cold, gray waters of the north Atlantic Ocean, laying their eggs in the sunwashed shallows of the coastal-river headwaters.

Tagging experiments have confirmed the barely plausible belief that, after leaving their natal streams as 8-inch smolt and crossing the trackless, gray expanse of the Atlantic Ocean to feed on nutrient-rich krill off the coast of Greenland, they find their way unerringly back to the very pool in which they were born. Just how they accomplish this feat of instinctive navigation continues to mystify man.

The Atlantic salmon knows no proprietary boundaries; though its range has shrunk because of human interference, it continues to inhabit virtually the entire Atlantic arena. In Europe, salmon still run strong in the rivers of Spain; the

The St. Jean River in Quebec yielded this 10-pound Atlantic which is displayed by a salmon fishing guide.

Atlantic Coast Salmon

British Isles boast fishable stocks of Atlantics; a few salmon tenaciously cling to the last unfettered rivers of France, and while hydroelectric development has barricaded many of the once-great salmon rivers of Sweden and Finland, salmon continue to seek out the rivers of Norway and the Soviet Union's Kola Peninsula.

North America, particularly eastern Canada, is still the stronghold of the Atlantic salmon, though historical records show that their range was even greater when European explorers first set foot in the New World. The diaries of these dauntless adventurers suggest that salmon may have run rivers as far south as the Delaware. British explorer Henry Hudson in 1609 reported seeing Atlantic salmon in "great store" when he explored what is now the Hudson River flowing past New York City. The Connecticut River, farther north, was said to have extensive runs of fish weighing 20 to 40 pounds.

Sadly, Atlantic salmon disappeared from most of the southern streams; ambitious restocking operations on the Connecticut River have restored a trace of the once-great runs. The most astounding success, however, has been on Maine rivers like the Penobscot where its pools fill with some 3,000 anadromous Atlantic salmon, thanks to restoration programs.

Eastern Canada boasts some 400 scheduled salmon rivers, among them legendary streams like Nova Scotia's Margaree and St. Mary's River, New Brunswick's Miramichi and Restigouche Rivers, the Humber in insular Newfoundland and the Eagle in Labrador. Quebec has its own fair share of notable and famous Atlantic salmon rivers—the Grand Cascapedia, the Matapedia, the Moisie and the George. In fact, at the northern edge of its range, natural barriers impede the Atlantic salmon's distribution. Beyond Hopedale, the Labrador escarpment denies the fish access to upriver spawning beds; water temperature forms as effective a barrier on most other northern rivers. North America's northernmost Atlantic salmon rivers are the George, Whale, Koksoak and Leaf which flow into Ungava Bay in northern Quebec.

Life Cycle
Throughout their range, past and present, the life and death patterns for Atlantics differ little. After hatching in the

sunwashed, headwater riffles in April, the alevin tarry in the safety of the fine gravel for several weeks until the yolk sac absorbs completely, sometime in late May or early June. Eager to feed on the stream's microscopic creatures, the 2-inch fry wiggle up through their protective nest of pebbles, the first of many critical journeys which weed out the weak from the strong. Called fingerlings, the free-swimming fry feed constantly and double their size in a matter of weeks.

At slightly over 3 inches in length, parr markings consisting of a series of 11 alternating light and dark vertical bands with a single red dot between each, develop along the sides of the fingerlings. During this period in the life of an Atlantic salmon, the parr are prized items on the menu for a host of rapacious creatures. Kingfishers, herons and mergansers are foremost among the predators, but native brook trout and other fish found in the waters also consider parr a delicious snack. The total losses are staggering; out of the 8,000 eggs laid by the hen salmon, only 50 will survive beyond the parr stage to go to sea.

Normally, the parr spend at least the first summer and winter in the stream before smolting—the process during which they gradually readapt themselves for life in the open ocean. The availability of food seems to be the critical factor determining the initial in-river segment. On rivers where food is scarce they often linger as many as six years in freshwater, but if food is abundant, smoltification sometimes takes place after only a year. Typically, the 5- to 10-inch parr make their way gradually downstream to the mouth of the river during May and June, two years after hatching. As they travel, the camouflage parr marks fade to an overall bright, silvery color.

Adapting To The Sea

A smolt school spends a few days getting used to the saltiness of the ocean, then they disappear out into the open Atlantic. In the mid-1960s, drift-netters working off the west coast of Greenland discovered one of the major feeding grounds used by North American stocks of Atlantic salmon and, more recently, a secondary feeding ground was found off the coast of Labrador. Here, the young salmon grow rapidly, gorging themselves on crustaceans, caplin and other marine life.

There exists no fast and fixed rule regarding the amount of

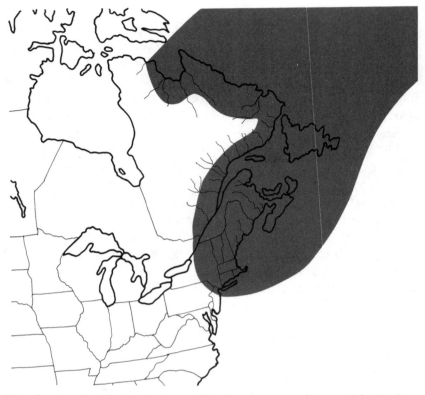

Prime locations for Atlantic salmon are within the gray zone on this map of the Northeast and eastern Canadian provinces. Rivers of eastern Quebec, the Maritime Provinces and the upper Northeastern United States provide excellent sportfishing for Atlantics.

time that salmon spend at sea. As a matter of fact, some smolt venture no further than the brackish water of the estuary before joining the incoming runs of salmon for the journey back upstream. Others linger up to four years on the feeding grounds, returning as big sea maidens that weigh over 25 pounds.

These, however, are the exceptions. In a normal salmon population, roughly two-thirds of the fish return as two-sea-winter fish weighing about 12 pounds, one-third may return as one-sea-winter fish (called grilse) weighing 3 to 5 pounds and the balance returns as three-sea-winter maidens weighing about 18 pounds. River conditions and generations of commercial netting, which selectively removed the multiple-sea-winter fish, may vary these proportions, but the three distinct runs represent a unique survival strategy ensuring that no single

Complete Angler's Library

generation is ever totally eliminated because of adverse conditions or calamity. To further reinforce this survival strategy, North America's grilse runs generally end on the Labrador feeding grounds. Time does not permit them to journey to the West Greenland feeding grounds, but at the same time, nature also insures that, should a major catastrophe take place on one of the feeding grounds, another population survives to repopulate the rivers.

First Runs Come Early

The first salmon en route to their spawning beds enter freshwater following the spring runoffs, usually sometime between mid-May and mid-June through most of eastern Canada. However, there are some late rivers where the salmon show up in August, particularly those at the northern extremes of their range. Large, mature salmon eager to reach the redds arrive first; grilse usually follow. They congregate in resting pools where the cool, oxygen-rich water can sustain them until the days begin to shorten and autumn turns the hardwood ridges into a riot of color.

Through this wait, the fasting salmon undergo a slow metamorphosis. The plump, dime-bright flanks of the big hens begin to tarnish to a dull copper color after only a few weeks in freshwater and the precious load of roe begins to swell. But, while the transformation of the hen is subtle, that of the male is far more startling. After a month in freshwater, the male's flanks turn to a burnished copper; in addition, the lower jaw slowly develops into a grotesque hook or kype to intimidate interlopers and impress potential conquests.

Through the dog days of August, the salmon respond to falling water levels and rising water temperatures by congregating motionless in the river's deep pools, gasping for what little oxygen the riffle can deliver. When September's rains finally bring the river back to life, the fish resume their journey to the headwaters, urged on by the shortening hours of daylight. By late October, they throng the pools closest to the shallow beds of pebbles where they themselves were born years before.

Sometime in early November, the female salmon initiates the ceremony. She turns on her side and, with powerful strokes of her tail, sweeps out a shallow depression in the streambed.

Once the nest is made, both the male and female hover over it, side by side. While she deposits about 800 eggs, the male fertilizes them by secreting a cloud of milt. Once this is done, the female once again turns on her side and thrashes her tail to sweep pebbles into the nest, covering the eggs.

Makes Several Nests

A hen salmon carries between 700 and 800 eggs per pound of body weight, so a 10-pound fish will carry between 7,000 and 8,000 eggs, each about the size of a pea. She makes as many as 10 nests to ensure that, even if some of the nests are destroyed, a portion of her young will survive.

Neither parent fish remains to protect the redd; instead, they head downriver to either spend the winter in one of the deep pools, or, if time permits before freeze-up, they go out into the river's estuary. From the time the salmon enter the river, until the time they leave, they do not eat and, as a result they become gaunt replicas of the silver, sleek fish they once were. In their weakened state after spawning, the salmon are prey to any number of fish-eating predators capable of taking large fish. Nevertheless, a few salmon do survive to spawn again, and, in rarer cases, a third time.

These multiple spawners can attain weights of over 50 pounds—the world-record, rod-and-reel Atlantic salmon is a 79-pound fish taken on Norway's Tana River. The accepted North American sporting record is a 55-pound fish from Quebec's Grand Cascapedia River. Reputedly, larger salmon have been caught and released in recent years: A big male multiple-spawner estimated at about 65 pounds was brought to boat on the Restigouche River in 1989 and another estimated at 72 pounds was released on the same river in 1990.

Freshwater Salmon

Though kin to the anadromous Atlantic salmon, landlocked salmon spend their entire lives in freshwater, shunning saltwater and its riches even when they have ready access to the sea. At one time, scientists considered them a distinct species or, at the very least, subspecifically distinct and named the fish found in the watersheds north of the St. Lawrence River Valley watershed *Salmo ouananiche*; those south of the St. Lawrence

Atlantic Salmon

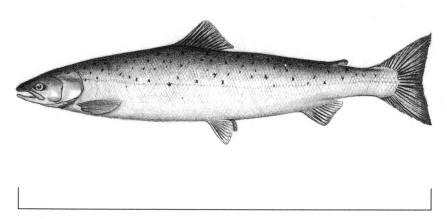

Anadromous Atlantic salmon, and those inhabiting deep lakes, have silvery sides, with irregular black marks. Landlocked Atlantics have spots larger than the anadromous salmon and possibly with halos. Atlantics may resemble brown trout, but their tails slightly fork and they have no spots on the adipose fin.

were listed as *Salmo sebago*, after the Maine lake in which large, freshwater salmon were abundant. Lately, however, taxonomists have concluded that the ouananiche of French Canada, the Sebago salmon of Maine and the once-abundant salmon of Lake Ontario are one and the same fish—the glamorous anadromous Atlantic salmon.

Though the distinctive taxonomy has been stripped away, anglers continue to keep the terminologies alive. There does indeed appear to be discernible differences between the fish. It's possible that these differences are primarily a function of environment rather than genetics. Along the Labrador coast, there are populations of landlocked salmon which have unobstructed access to the open seas and prefer to remain in their freshwater surroundings.

This single, innate preference for the sweet taste of freshwater raises questions about the origins of landlocked salmon. There's no controversy as to the common roots of both anadromous and freshwater salmon. On the other hand, there's no easy resolution to the riddle as to which came first. Its name suggests that landlocked salmon evolved from anadromous salmon. These fish adapted to life in a freshwater environment after finding their access to the sea barricaded by glaciers and upheavals of the earth's crust.

Maybe so, but it's entirely possible, too, that anadromous fish developed from original freshwater populations during a bygone era when the land was in the grip of the Ice Ages. Four massive glaciers rumbled south across the Canadian Shield; the first three rumbled over the elemental bedrock of the fire-formed Precambrian Shield. The last one, the Wisconsin Glacier, ground southward about 100,000 years ago and held the land in its icy grip for 60,000 years. When it withdrew, some 38,000 years before Christ, it had put the final brush strokes to the land of the landlocked salmon.

Trapped By Glaciers

Popular theory suggests that the retreat of the Wisconsin Glacier trapped anadromous Atlantic salmon in many lakes and rivers of northeastern North America; hence, the landlocked salmon. Yet, the theory is shaky because, throughout its natural range, no obstacles capable of shackling the irrepressible spirit of *Salmo salar* existed.

A second theory suggests that all Atlantic salmon were once denizens of brawling rivers and clear, crystalline pools, and that the advance of the last Ice Age created conditions in the rivers unsuitable to large salmon populations. In order to survive, many salmon were forced downstream and eventually into the sea, while those that could, remained in freshwater.

The salmon which retreated before the encroaching ice gradually adapted to a marine interval with physiological modifications which made it possible to survive in saltwater. A period of 60,000 years—the life of the Wisconsin Glacier—is more than sufficient time for such an evolutionary change. As long as run-off from the leading edge of the ice field provided suitable, though restrained, freshwater spawning habitat, there was no need to evolve a marine reproductive strategy.

Hence, we have sea-run—or anadromous—salmon which roam the food-rich Atlantic Ocean by choice and fight their way into the shallow riffles of freshwater rivers to procreate. And, we have freshwater salmon which live in inland rivers and lakes by choice, not because some Precambrian upheaval has barricaded their access to the sea. They are landlocked only in the sense that nature has not adapted them to live in saltwater.

The most telling difference between the sea-run and freshwater salmon is size. Deprived of the vast riches of the open ocean, landlocked salmon must content themselves with the meager fare of the rivers and lakes. On this diet of aquatic insects, smelt and other subsurface creatures, the fish grow slowly—far more slowly than their sea-going kin. A 22-pound, 8-ounce landlocked salmon taken in Lake Sebago, Maine, in 1907 is recognized as the world record for these fish. It's just a matter of time until that record falls. Already, we've come close to doing so several times, most notably in 1982 when a 21-pound, 6-ounce landlock was caught in Quebec's Lake Tremblant. Biologists monitoring Tremblant salmon on the Caché River spawning beds say they have seen 30-pound fish.

Sea-Run Parentage

Purists argue that the Tremblant fish should not actually be considered true landlocked salmon since they, like the salmon stocked in many lakes and rivers throughout eastern North America, are actually the direct progeny of sea-run Atlantic salmon. These fish adopt habits identical to landlocked salmon, but grow faster and bigger, habitat permitting.

The adaptability of anadromous salmon to a landlocked existence was proven in restocking operations on Lake Champlain, a long, narrow body of water that stretches from the Canadian border halfway down between New York and Vermont. At one time, great numbers of salmon ran tributaries such as the Au Sable, the Bouquet, Missisquoi, Lamoille and Winooski. But, by the mid-1800s, they dwindled and disappeared entirely. A century later, at a time when coho and chinook salmon were the darlings of fish and game authorities and anglers alike, fisheries biologists in Vermont and New York decided to restore indigenous Atlantic salmon stocks in Lake Ontario (as outlined in Chapter 1).

Is There A Difference?

These stocking programs raise the questions: What really is the difference between anadromous and freshwater Atlantic salmon? Should there really be any differentiation between

This angler has just nabbed a small, landlocked salmon. The fish was taken from Lake Memphremagog in Quebec.

them at all? Essentially, their life histories are identical—both mature from smolt to breeders on the abundance provided by large bodies of water, be it lake, inland sea or open ocean. Then, at maturity, both enter their natal streams to spawn, and their offspring spend the first year or two in the stream before leaving for the expanse of open water. The difference is anadromous salmon seek the gray waters of the Atlantic Ocean while landlocked salmon stay in freshwater.

Though landlocked salmon still exist through much of the former range, native, self-sustaining populations are a rare commodity in all but the most remote waters. Maine's landlocked salmon fishery is a major drawing card in the angling community, especially Aroostook County waters, as well as the waters of the upper Penobscot and Grand Lake. Neighboring New Hampshire also boasts landlocked salmon fishing, as does Vermont and New York states, mostly by virtue of restocking operations in Lake Champlain. Other scattered populations exist throughout New England, Canada's Maritime provinces and southern Quebec; some in waters where the species is indigenous, many in waters where it is not, but by and large maintained by regular stocking programs.

Farther north, indigenous populations of landlocked salmon continue to thrive because the impact of man's interference is buffered because of the region's remoteness. In Quebec, the watersheds that feed Lake St. Jean in the Saguenay region are home to native landlocked salmon, as are the tributaries of the Manicouagan drainage. These fish also frequent watersheds of the Gulf of St. Lawrence's north shore, around the corner into Labrador and up the coast as far as Hopedale. Many waters in the Churchill Reservoir drainages are home to lightly fished populations of landlocked salmon. These fish also inhabit countless lakes of insular Newfoundland. In northern Quebec, most tributaries to Ungava Bay support landlocks, too.

Salmon Angling
Equipment

4

Salmon Gear—Rods And Reels

L ike a talented illusionist's magic wand, today's sport anglers wave rods and reels with a special touch in an attempt to entice a variety of fish species into hitting the bait, be it live or artificial. Without the rod-and-reel combination, fishermen have nothing—no way to lure or catch their intended quarry. Selection of this important equipment should not be taken lightly.

Equipment progression within the industry has come a long way since the days of Izaak Walton. Fishing has become very specialized. It includes pursuit of specific species, as well as the particular method of pursuit (i.e., trolling, casting, jigging) that will be utilized. Finding the right rod and reel for your needs depends on many factors, including personal preference. Identify what it is that you'll be using the rod and reel for, and then research it thoroughly by talking with fellow fishermen, reading available materials on performance and selection in product review sections in *North American Fisherman* and other sportfishing-oriented magazines, and attending fishing equipment seminars or in-store promotion events. These are ways to help you make that all-important decision on the right rod-and-reel combination.

Of course, you can get more technical information if you want. The rod's performance is determined by the method of construction, mandrel design, fibers selected and size and shape of material pattern. The more technical your research is, the

Development of specialized tackle for special situations includes rods for downrigging, other high-stress situations and noodling. From left: the Triton Down Rigger rod with Shimano's 200FS Triton Speedmaster reel; the Fenwick Eagle Graphite E120S rod with Penn 420SS spinning reel; and, Fenwick's Eagle Graphite E90C H-2 rod with Daiwa's 600M Millionaire II Series, high-speed baitcasting reel.

Salmon Gear—Rods And Reels   55

easier it will be to understand differences in rods. However, this much research is not essential in making a good decision.

The important thing is that you make a selection that will best meet your needs. When you specialize in taking salmon, your rod-and-reel selections must be based on both the size and power of these popular fish.

Just as important is the type of fishing line that you select. Once again, the type of line (pound-test, strength and stretching capabilities) must be tailored to the type of angling activity. Light line can be run off downriggers with the right type of rod-and-reel package. Heavier line might be needed if you're running divers; and, if you don't have a lot of experience and are using a charter service, medium to heavy line might be the best choice.

Without a line you can rely upon, though, and a good rod-and-reel combination, your fishing (and attitude) could suffer correspondingly. NAFC members who are getting youngsters involved should resist the habit of handing down old gear. A youngster's frustration with equipment can lead to the child losing interest in fishing.

Great Lakes Rods And Reels

Improvements in rods and reels during the past 25 years have been astounding, and the future in tackle improvements looks to be spectacular.

Great Lakes salmon fishing's strong suit has been the development and use of downriggers. During the early stages of downriggers, the immediate needs of trollers were not addressed. Early rod-and-reel design did not anticipate the introduction of downriggers. However, it wasn't long before the industry caught up to, and surpassed, the technological level of these new tools.

Downrigger Rods

Your personal preference, based on your confidence level, will dictate your choice in rods for use with downriggers. There are several considerations, including the rod butt, number of guides and rod length.

The butt is important for several reasons. The length should be adequate so that the rod will fit solidly into a rod holder.

These rods are built with downrigger use in mind. All have the longer butts that fit securely into the holders. They also have the popular round grip for the angler when taking the rod in hand to bring in the fish.

Cork is a very popular grip, but wears quicker than foam.

"Round grips have pretty much been standard for the industry," says Mike Fine, press and public relations director for Berkley, a major rod manufacturer. "One of the innovations for downrigger rods is the use of a triangular grip. Not only is this more comfortable, but there's not as much strain on your grip. This, in turn, will help you keep pressure on the fish with the rod, instead of the fish applying pressure on you. You have more control over the fish situation. With your confidence level up, you'll catch more fish."

The number of guides is important because it's essential that the guides keep the line off the rod itself. "If you've got a two-piece rod, put it together and flex it on a floor carpet," Fine says. "Look to see if there's enough guides to handle the line. If you're still unsure, thread your line through and bend the rod into a parabolic curve. If the line touches the rod, there aren't enough guides."

Most rods are graphite composite, with a good number also made of fiberglass because of the material's lower cost and durability. When selecting a downrigger rod, you should be aware that lightness and sensitivity aren't as important as durability and flexibility. Because a downrigger rod is under constant pressure, the rod's capacity to withstand this pressure should also be part of your selection decision.

A good, fast-action tip is another important factor. It should be sensitive enough for fighting smaller fish in a more sporting fashion, as well as forgiving when novice salmon anglers are reeling in Great Lakes kings.

The perfect rod for use with downriggers probably would be a medium-action rod with 10 to 12 guides, an overall length of 7½ to 9½ feet, a long rod butt and a comfortable, foam grip. The most popular reel for trolling the Great Lakes for salmon is a large, heavy-duty levelwind, featuring a high retrieve ratio, good line capacity and a reliable, smooth, drag system. Levelwind reels spread the line evenly over the spool, and provide enough line capacity for handling those feisty salmon both in the spring and fall.

A good drag is necessary for Great Lakes salmon fishing. You must keep pressure on the fish, but not so much that the line breaks or the lure pulls from the fish's mouth. Drags are normally adjusted for the size of the fish and the fishing technique being used. Drags provide resistance at the spool which creates friction. Poorly constructed reels will not last during the 100-yard run of a large salmon. It's only a matter of time before they freeze and break, another casualty in the battle with large salmon. Most reels are made of cast aluminum or graphite. Weight and weatherability are important considerations, but looks and personal preference are, too.

Downrigger reels should have a free-spool mode for letting line out, and a spool clicker as a third mode between the normal drag and free spooling. The clicker is handy when lowering downrigger weight to a predetermined depth.

Choice of monofilament line to use with downriggers depends upon the season, and the angler's proficiency with a rod. Eight- to 12-pound-test line for spring fishing in the Great Lakes is often more than adequate, especially when working in the season's clearer water. However, charter skippers usually will compromise with a choice of 14- to 17-pound-test line because it is more forgiving for customers who may not handle a rod well. Come fall, though, line of as much as 20-pound test may be used to tackle the larger, more mature fish.

It's important to check periodically for nicks and frays in the line. Salmon will test tackle limits. Any weaknesses in the line, knots and terminal tackle will be brought out by a powerful fish. A reel with good line capacity that allows you a good line supply on the spool to strip off when needed is a necessity, and don't take chances with line quality, use a premium line. After all, the line is the only link between you and the fish.

Dipsy-Diver Rods

These rods are but one example of the specialized rods being used for fishing the Great Lakes. Longer and stiffer than their downrigger counterparts, these rods are 9 to 10 feet in length. For diving plane fishing, rods need a flexible tip and a heavy butt. A heavier rod is needed because of the additional pull of the diver being dragged through deep water.

One reel which is ideally suited to diver fishing has a line-counter feature that tells you exactly how much line you have out. With the line-counter, you can repeat the depth at which your lure took a fish. Consistency is important, especially on those days when you're really having to work for fish. Details such as lead lengths or distance of the lure behind the boat can make all the difference in catching fish and being able to repeat the fish-catching performance. Was the fish taken on a turn? What was the boat's speed? What direction was I going? All these questions and more should be asked, and the important factor of the lure's distance behind the boat can be easily determined with a line-counter reel.

Line test for diving plane fishing is usually in the 15- to 20-pound class. Use a premium brand of line with very little stretch so the release will trip when there's a fish on.

Lead-Core Rod

Similar to a diver rod, rods for use with lead-core line must

A large-capacity, heavy-duty reel and a stout rod are required when using lead-core line. This angler is using this setup while fishing from a Great Lakes charter boat. Flatlining with lead-core line can be effective when downriggers aren't working.

handle heavier weight and constant trolling pressure. An 8½- to 9½-foot rod is usually preferred.

Again, line-counter reels are ideal for lead-core-line trolling. If you don't have a line-counter reel, any reel big enough to have good spool capacity to handle the diameter and the amount of line that's let out will be fine.

Lead-core lines, which come in different test weights, can be extremely effective in the Great Lakes when run out some distance behind the boat. This is especially true on days when the water is clear, and fish are near the surface. This is a situation when action on the downriggers is normally slow, so using lead-core lines will help stimulate fishing action.

You'll need at least 200 yards of monofilament backing on your spool which is followed by lead-core line. One of the popular lead-core weights is 25-pound test. Fifty yards of 25-pound-test, lead-core line will put the lure about 20 feet below the surface; 100 yards will put it about 40 feet down. The finishing touch on this fish-catching package is 50 to 100 feet of leader, preferably 15- to 20-pound test.

When trolling with lead-core line, be sure all the lead core is off the spool and submerged. This is when it will work best for you. However, do not use this line if you're in heavy boat traffic, for obvious reasons. The line can be very effective in catching 16-foot boats, as well as large salmon.

Drift-Fishing Rod

If you're looking for a drift-fishing rod, consider something with more graphite content. Not only is the rod lighter, but it will also be more sensitive than comparable rods with less graphite. The sensitivity will be important when you're using bottom-bouncing tackle.

Optimum rod length is determined by several factors including personal preference, boat size and the weight of line you want to run. The longer the rod, the lighter the line you can use. This is a reason for the increased popularity of 10- to 12-foot noodle rods. In addition to levelwind reels, spinning or other baitcasting reels can also be used, especially in river situations. Be extremely careful with spinning reels, though. The drag must adjust properly, and you must know when a fish is taking line out. If you start cranking while line is being taken out or just if it is still, one full turn of the handle can amount to 2½ to 3 feet of line twist. Let the rod fight the fish, keeping the rodtip up at between 10 and 12 o'clock. Don't turn the handle until you can gain line back on a tired fish. Spinning is definitely a finesse-style of fishing when drifting, or even casting from shore. It requires your utmost attention at all times.

When fishing from shore, however, it's probably the most popular gear among land-bound anglers because more area can be covered with spinning gear.

Jigging Rods

For Great Lakes jigging, most anglers prefer a shorter, stiffer rod allowing more control for the angler, and providing better feel for the hit. A longer, whippier rod doesn't transmit strikes as well.

A line-weight rule of thumb for jiggers is to move up one line-test class. If you normally fish with 8-pound test, bump it up to 10-pound test for jigging. Variables to be considered in making this decision include depth and water temperature variation.

Reel preferences will vary, but whatever reel you use must have a smooth drag. When they hit, Great Lakes salmon generally do a good imitation of a freight train, and puny reels with inconsistent drags just won't stand the punishment.

Western Rods And Reels

Pacific Coast salmon fishermen begin assembling a wide assortment of rods and reels shortly after their first few fishing trips. Once bitten by the "salmon bug," fishermen break out in a rash of gear that matches tackle and line to the size of salmon they choose to pursue and, also, the type of water in which they will fish.

For spinning outfits, fiberglass and some graphite rods from 6- to 7½-feet long are ideal for sight-casting to resident coho in sounds, straits, estuaries and bays. The same rods function equally well for catching humpies and coho salmon in West Coast rivers. Wear-resistant guides and tip eyes are needed for long life and reliable service. Reels should be high-quality mills capable of holding 90 to 125 yards of monofilament, testing 4, 6 or 8 pounds. A smoothly functioning line drag is critical.

Increase the spinning-rod size as the waters fished and quarry sought get larger, and you will top out with a rod 8- to 9½-feet long, having a cork or closed-cell foam butt that reaches the angler's elbow. Reels swell accordingly, with line capacity of 150 to 175 yards of 12- to 18-pound test needed.

In British Columbia, anglers favor longer rods, from 10 to 11½ feet in length, and generally use centre-pin reels hung under the lengthy cork butt.

Graphite, fiberglass and some boron rods of 5 and 6 weight are commonly used in fly fishing for resident salmon in big waters and fishing smaller species of salmon in rivers. Sink-tip and weight-forward lines terminate in leader strength of 3 to 6 pounds. Reels must be large enough to spool on 80 to 100 yards

Anglers mooching salmon can either hold the rod as this angler is doing or fish the rod from a holder on the rail as also shown in this photo. Mooching outfits are a specialty item used primarily on the West Coast.

of backing in addition to fly line. As you fish for larger salmon in rivers and straits, fly-rod sizes increase to 9 weight, and sometimes 10. These systems with correspondingly larger reels must accommodate more backing to sustain longer runs.

Levelwind, multiplying reels holding 100 to 140 yards of 12- to 20-pound-test monofilament generally are matched with fiberglass, some graphite or a few boron rods of slightly under 8 feet to over 9 feet for most salmon angling. Butt length generally equals the length of the angler's hand and forearm, and rods normally have a fore-grip for two-handed battles. When freshwater reels are used in saltwater areas, they should be rinsed well to prevent rusting. (Pack a quart, plastic jug of detergent-water mix and a rag. Soak your reels in the mixture and rinse in freshwater; then, put lures used that day in the jar and shake well before rinsing.)

Two types of reels hold sway. Reels intended for freshwater-use must be capable of laying out casts of 60 to 100 feet with free-spooling accuracy and trouble-free operation. Saltwater reels are not normally cast, so their strongest feature should be starwheel drags that operate smoothly.

Salmon Gear—Rods And Reels

Specialty rigs such as mooching rods are a distinctively West Coast item. Most are fiberglass, measuring 8 to 9 feet in length. Their tips are light enough to betray a nibbling salmon; then, the rods progress into increasing belly strength and strong butt sections.

Other special-use salmon rods are borrowed from the bass angler's world. Popping sticks or flippin' rods of 6 to 7½ feet in length are matched with levelwind, starwheel-drag reels for use in light jigging on lakes, reservoirs and at river mouths.

Stout, fiberglass rods with conventional guides are favored for use in trolling with monofilament lines up to 35 or 40 pounds in breaking strength. These are called "boat rods." Commonly, they are 6 to 7½ feet long and may also sometimes be used for trolling lead-core line. Large-capacity reels holding 250 or more yards of line are standard. Reel features may include levelwind, but more often do not. Sturdy, efficient drags are essential.

For wire line, anglers use special reels. These are high-sided, large-capacity aluminum or plated-steel winches. Most have a release lever for letting out line and a sturdy drag system. Rods must have roller guides and tips to help lessen line abrasion.

Atlantic Salmon

Fly fishing is the general rule for fishing on all scheduled Atlantic salmon rivers of eastern North America—a restriction dictated both by custom and law. Right from the beginnings of Atlantic salmon angling in the mid-1800s, sportfishermen cast flies across crystalline pools according to traditions brought to North American rivers by British gentry.

At core, while the basics of salmon angling have changed little, the greenheart poles and horsehair lines cast by 19th century anglers have been replaced with space age materials of the 20th century. From time to time, you might still come across a traditionalist using a fine-split bamboo rod on a North American salmon river, but virtually everybody today has switched to graphite—or at the very least, fiberglass—rods. Even the 14- to 16-foot, two-handed rods commonly encountered on European rivers are rarely seen here.

Virtually any fly rod from 2 weight through 12 weight is capable of subduing a salmon. However, an 8- or 9-weight,

9-foot graphite fly rod best covers all eventualities likely to be encountered on a salmon stream. Bear in mind that accuracy of presentation is far more critical than delicacy of presentation. The rod must be able to cast wet flies from size 12 single low water to size 2/0 double, and it should drive a bulky, long-shanked, spun-deerhair Bomber out across the water into a stiff breeze with equal ease. And, the angler must be able to lay out cast after cast, hour after hour, without tiring.

Good advice to anyone planning to take up—and enjoy—Atlantic salmon fishing is to stick with the half-dozen or so top graphite fly rods on the market today. Try as many of these as you can streamside to get the feel of the particular and individual action of each to find which best suits your casting style and temperament. Fishing acquaintances and friends are usually more than happy to let you try their rods during the course of a fishing trip. Hefting a rod in a sporting goods store will tell you very little about the differing personalities of the handful of top rods.

Need Fighting Butt

As far as hardware is concerned, a good salmon rod must have a fighting butt. Some come with a permanent butt, others with a detachable butt or fighting butt extension. While the detachable butt is most often used, rummaging through your fishing vest for the butt can be a minor inconvenience in the heat of the fight. Most permanent fighting butts are too small to fulfill their purpose, and the extension butts eventually bend out of shape and no longer slide in and out easily.

Another feature to look for is an uplocking rather than downlocking reel seat. First of all, this serves to position the reel slightly higher on the butt of the rod, reducing the likelihood of it catching in the shirt, vest or rain jacket during the salmon's initial hard run—at least until you can find your detachable butt. Secondly, anglers tend to develop some sloppy casting habits over the years; among them is gripping the rod close to the reel. On a downlocking reel seat, the locking nut tends to work loose. An uplocking reel seat positions the hand squarely on the cork handle.

In Atlantic salmon fishing, a reel is more than just a convenient place to store line; it is actually an integral

For challenging salmon, a good, heavy-duty reel is a must. The reel should have line capacity in the 150- to 200-yard range, and a smooth, dependable brake system. Lightweight reels just won't stand up to the punishment of a strong run.

component in the strategy to subdue these fish. It should have capacity enough to hold, with room to spare, the fly line and, at the very minimum, 100 yards of 20-pound Dacron backing. On small rivers, you may never find yourself wishing you had more, but on larger waters and big-fish rivers a 200-yard reserve of backing can save the day.

A salmon reel must also have a solid brake system. Early on, anglers used primarily British reels with a spring-loaded ratchet drag that did little more than keep the spool from overrunning. Now, there are American-made reels that boast fancy, disc-drag systems. Both take salmon; the latter do so more effectively. The manufacturer's statement that the reel can stop a runaway freight matters little unless you're in runaway-freight-train country. What you need is a smooth, dependable drag with

Complete Angler's Library

minimal start-up load. You will probably never want to apply more than 4 or 5 pounds of brake on any salmon, at any time.

Exposed Rim

A lot of fuss is made over the exposed rim of a salmon reel, but it may be an overrated issue. If the reel has a good drag to begin with, you won't need to supplement by applying palm pressure on the rim; that's something that's talked about a lot but rarely done in the heat of battle. As a matter of fact, some of the elegant older salmon reels like the vom Hoffe and its many imitators have no exposed rim.

On the other hand, not enough fuss is made over the click-out ratchets. The characteristic song of the old British salmon reel is as much a part of salmon angling as the diamond-studded leap of a salmon on a sun-bright morning. But the clicker has a useful function, as well, since it allows a guide at the ready with the net to follow the progress of the battle without having to turn around to see what the angler is doing.

Landlocked Salmon

Though the fly patterns used to catch landlocked salmon are considerably different from those used for anadromous Atlantic salmon, the rest of the equipment does double duty. Graphite rods 9 feet long capable of handling 6- to 8-pound-test lines are recommended. However, you may, on some waters, particularly lakes, rely more heavily on sink-tip lines, occasionally even full-sinking lines for lake fishing.

By far, the majority of landlocked salmon fishing, however, is not done with fly rod in hand, but rather by casting lures or trolling, as covered elsewhere in this book. Medium-action spinning rods loaded with 8-pound-test monofilament are ideal for spinning, as well as most Atlantic Coast trolling situations.

5

Coastal Salmon Gear

Wen selecting the most effective and pleasing-to-use combination of rod, reel, rigging and terminal gear for use in the Northwest, it's important to consider the types of fishing. The bulk of Pacific Coast salmon angling is done in big waters short of the entry of fish runs into their natal streams. Here are some of the many proven uses of equipment to hook a West Coast, big-water salmon:

Surface To 40 Feet

Sight-casting may be one of the hottest, most exciting but little-known ways of fishing big waters of the Northwest for salmon. Especially effective for schools of young "resident" coho in sounds, bays, estuaries and inlets, sight-casting is practiced with light- to medium-weight fly rods or spinning rigs and shrimp-imitating flies. Best timing for this interesting fishery is late February through May.

A No. 5 to No. 7 fly rod outfit, with matched sinking-tip line and leader tapering to about 3 pounds test weight, works great for casting to feeding coho of 2 to 5 pounds. A good 7-foot, spinning outfit carrying 80 to 100 yards of 6-pound-test line may be used with a clear, plastic float partially filled with water to give the rig casting weight. Shrimp flies tied with fluorescent chenille in chartreuse or green colors over pink or orange bodies draw eager strikes.

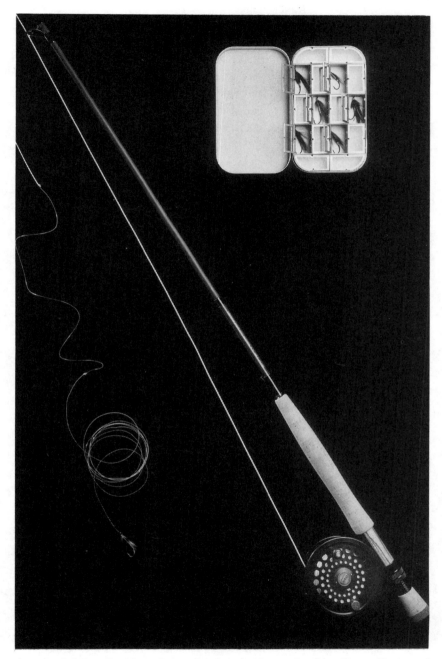

A quality 8½-foot, 7- to 8-weight, graphite fly rod with a good, solid reel is an effective tool for catching salmon in West Coast rivers. A selection of wet flies that has proven effective in your area completes your fly-fishing arsenal.

Having found schooled, feeding coho by watching bird action or searching for less-visible finning and tail movements near rips and eddies, anglers cast beyond the fish and retrieve in inch-short to foot-long twitches to attract coho to the hook.

Flatlining is surface fishing with no weight or nearly unencumbered bare line to a lure or bait trolled behind a boat. At most, ¼- to ½-ounce keel sinkers may be attached 3 to 4 feet ahead of a streamer fly, bucktail, light spoon, spinner or whole herring for trolling just below the water's surface film. Medium to heavy fly rods, baitcasting rigs or large spinning outfits are used in wide, lower stretches of rivers and between their mouths and the ocean. Strikes can be highly visible, while the ensuing battles often are very exciting man-to-fish direct confrontations.

From just below the surface to 30 or 40 feet, shallow subsurface angling utilizing the same rods with the addition of crescent-shaped salmon sinkers of 2 to 5 ounces in both trolling and mooching techniques produces good catches.

Semi-Deep, 40 To 100 Feet

Jigging can be handled with the same tackle used in shallower conditions and a handful of jigs and jigging spoons. Many sportfishermen, however, prefer special-purpose rods for light-tackle jigging and different rod models for deep jigging, as do fishermen in other parts of the country.

Getting Down ...

Downrigger fishing penetrates from near-surface to the murkiest depths at which salmon are taken. Short-armed manual or electric downriggers spool a heavy weight to a specific depth. The angler's line attaches to the downrigger weight or its wire with a release mechanism actuated by a strike. Since the angling line is separate from, and pops free of, the downrigger, anglers can enjoy weight-free battles with spunky salmon. Therefore, you can enjoy angling with your favorite salmon rod and reel and light lines of 10 to 18 pounds, testing your skill against the salmon's power.

... And Devious

Divers, planers and trolling boards put more strain on tackle than the techniques listed above, so sturdier rods and reels

Jigging Patterns

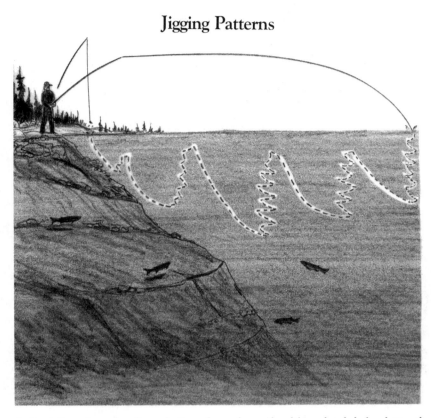

In jig-angling, the angler allows the jig to flutter down, then lifts and reels before letting the jig drop again. Strikes generally occur when the jig descends.

should be considered. Normally, medium-heavy baitcasting rigs are used and reels are large-capacity, starwheel drag, levelwind models. Monofilament of 15 to 30 pounds is recommended, depending on the size of fish you expect to encounter. Think positive. Be prepared for the big ones. You may wish you had when a big salmon snags your line and swims defiantly away.

Wire And Lead Core

Wire line and lead-core line fishing are extremely productive methods, but require specialized, oversize reels that are capable of holding several hundred yards of line. Your terminal tackle may be 350 to 400 or more feet from your rodtip when a strike occurs. Rods should be heavy-duty models equipped with roller guides and roller tips, since standard guides could be, and more than likely will be, very quickly abraded, grooved and ruined by these lines.

Which equipment is best for you? Fish several times with salmon-angling friends or take some charter or guided trips before you decide on this kind of equipment. Gearing up to fish with wire or lead-core line requires a significant investment.

Rainwear, Foot Gear

West Coast anglers have an appropriate saying about weather changes in their area. "If you don't like the weather now, wait a half-hour; it will change." Often, that change is to spitting rain squalls that sweep onto the shoreline and drop their load before climbing nearby mountains. Good rainwear is a critical fishing accessory, particularly from near the Columbia River north through Alaskan waters. Nobody can fish seriously or for any length of time when soaking wet and shivering.

Hooded, parka-style, fingertip-length raincoats are excellent choices for boaters and bank fishermen alike. This specific-length rainwear is extremely popular along the Pacific shoreline. It is long enough to overlap tops of hip boots, preventing run-off from going down into the boots, and short enough that river currents should not wrap it around the legs of wading anglers and tumble them downriver, as can happen with full-length raincoats.

Another good choice for boaters might be a two-piece rainsuit. Rainpants eliminate soggy bottoms and soaked pant legs, creature discomforts that can shorten fishing trips and greatly reduce enjoyment.

Deck shoes with non-skid rubber or composition soles are great boat shoes for sunny weather. Avoid leather soles, which are "accidents waiting for opportunity." A pair of weatherproof pacs or kneehighs works very well, and cut-off bottom halves of old hip boots are also commonly used on boats. Any of these will keep you dry and fishing in comfort.

It's smart, too, to pack an extra wool shirt or sweater on all salmon fishing trips. You can always climb into added warmth, but only if you have it with you.

Helpful Accessories

Every salmon angler should carry a good file or hook hone,

This angler, beaching a coho salmon, is wearing a multi-pocket vest. It allows him to keep virtually everything he needs within reach while keeping his hands free to fight fish.

to keep hook points sharp. You'll find several types available at tackle shops and marinas, or you might choose an ignition-point file, an inexpensive and easily found item that can be clipped or tied to your fishing vest or jacket.

Many Western anglers insist the correct way to create a needle-sharp point is to file from hook point toward the barb, using the same number of passes along either side of the point to obtain an evenly balanced sharpness. Three "cuts" are generally used. Two are on the lower, inside portions of the curved tip and back toward the barb slice and the third is a light brushing of the file over the point's top. Stroking toward point from barb is said to "pile up" metal at the tip, dulling the hook point.

Look closely at most pictures of Western-stream anglers and you will see a huge percentage of them wearing many-pocketed fishing vests or jackets. Like Ed McMahon might say to Johnny Carson, "*Everything* you need . . ." for a day or two of salmon angling can be packed in vest or jacket. It goes with you up and down the riverbank, but is easily shed into your car's trunk or shrugged off if you should step into water over your head. Baits are carried in bait canteens on a separate belt.

Coastal Salmon Gear

Boaters and plunkers need a landing net. A sturdy 26- to 30-inch hoop with an appropriately stout mesh net will do the job. Telescoping handles are standard with smaller nets, but commercial models for charter boats and large private sportfishing boats normally have long, fixed handles.

Proper salmon netting procedure leads the salmon to the net headfirst, preferably from an upcurrent angle, with the angler slackening rod pressure as his fish is brought over the net. At that point, the salmon generally noses into the bottom of the mesh. It is *not* wise to net a fish from the tail. A startled salmon, no matter how tired, seems to find one last spurt of energy when poked from the rear. The result is like holding a match to a jet plane's afterburner!

Wading anglers rely on a short, folding gaff to land Pacific salmon where they cannot be beached. After locking the gaff into extended position, hold the gaff point underwater parallel to the current at the river's edge and bring a salmon to it; then, rotate the gaff's point outward beneath the fish's pectoral area. Firmly pull upward with the gaff, sweeping the salmon from the water in one continuous motion.

In lieu of gaffing, a beaten salmon can be "tailed" for release by using a wool glove and grasping the fish firmly at the "wrist" of its tail holding it until your hook is freed.

When beaching salmon, it's best to bring the fish to the bank upstream from where you are standing, allowing the current to help strand it, rather than landing it downstream. If your leader snaps, you have a chance to pounce on a fish that current moves toward you. A salmon suddenly freed and washed downstream will most likely make it back into the river before you can do your grizzly-bear imitation.

Because salmon live in the water, the fly should be in the air as little as possible. A single backcast, though necessary, is already a waste of time; false casts, on the other hand, are unforgivable. False casting saps the angler's energy, reduces the amount of time that the fly is accessible to salmon and risks spooking the fish by false casting over them. For these reasons, insist on weight-forward lines; double taper lines are fine for delicate presentations on trout streams, but not for Atlantic salmon fishing. Weight-forward lines are available in a number of configurations, ranging from bass or saltwater tapers to

Basic Fly Line Shapes

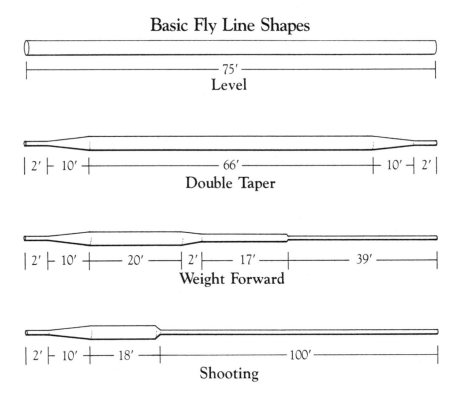

This diagram shows the difference in the basic fly line shapes. Floating lines are coated so they won't sink. Weight-forward lines are popular for most types of salmon fishing.

long-belly tapers. Bass tapers are often used to muscle big lures around on windy days and long-belly tapers on calm days.

Floating Lines

Almost all Atlantic salmon fishing should be done with full-floating line (even with wet flies) because the fish rise readily to take on or just under the surface. For the angler, this is a blessing since a floating line is relatively easy to lift off the water, compared to a sink-tip or full-sinking line. However, you should carry a sink-tip line with you on all salmon fishing trips and, because it can help you take fish when everything else fails, especially during periods of high or dirty water.

For most of the season, Atlantic salmon are not overly leader-shy, and the size of the tippet is determined primarily by the size of the fly—a No. 2 wet fly would hang limp on a 6-pound-test tippet and conversely a No. 10 fly would have no life tied to a 14-pound tippet. As a general rule, figure on using a 14-pound-test monofilament tippet with 2/0 to No. 2 flies, an 8- to 10-pound-test tippet with No. 2 to 8 flies and a 6- to 8-pound-test monofilament tippet with No. 6 to 8 flies. Leaders 9 to 12 feet in length are used most of the time, although during periods of low water, when the fish are easily spooked, a 14- and even 16-foot leader is advisable.

Knotted Or Knotless

Prepared salmon leaders, both knotted and knotless, can be purchased, but you can tie your own. Typically, a 12-foot leader for an 8- or 9-weight line starts with a 44-inch butt section of 30-pound-test monofilament. To this, blood knot a 40-inch section of 22-pound-test monofilament, followed by a 36-inch section of 17-pound-test monofilament. The tippet should be 24 inches long. Knotted leaders are preferred over the tapered knotless leaders because the knots turn the leader over better.

As far as ancillary equipment is concerned, you'll need a pair of waders for most Atlantic salmon fishing. Insist on felt bottoms to provide traction on the boulder-strewn rivers and the addition of studs gives even better footing. The advantage of boot-footed waders is the convenience of getting in and out of them, but stocking foot waders are more comfortable and offer less resistance in heavy current. Neoprene waders provide considerable insulation against cold water during early season fishing. In terms of cost, the regular booted waders are the best bargain, the neoprene stocking foot models are considerably more expensive and you'll need to buy wading boots and gaiters. Whatever the type, chest-high waders are strongly recommended because, no matter where you go, salmon rivers are always an inch or two deeper than the highest point of hip waders.

Add to this a belt to snug the waders tightly around your waist in case of an unforeseen dunking, a waterproof wading jacket in case of a downpour, a pair of polarized sunglasses to cut through the surface glare and a hat to fend off hooks gone astray in the wind. A good wading staff is a steadying friend when the current is strong and the footing uncertain.

A good pair of waders makes it easier to fish a stream effectively and safely. Many anglers prefer chest waders because they can work deeper water. However, a belt should be worn to keep chest waders from filling with water in the event of a fall.

Oh, and don't forget the insect repellent. Between mosquitoes, black flies and sand flies, there's rarely peace on a salmon river.

=6=

Salmon Gear—Electronic Aids

F ishing enhanced by the use of electronic gadgetry has helped raise the industry to a more sophisticated level. The Great Lakes has been the focal point for many of these electronic achievements, with anglers applying different types of knowledge relating to water and making them work for fish-catching or additional safety precautions on the water. Electronics have become the "seeing eye dog" for deep-water fishermen, whether it's to locate structure, fish, bait or thermoclines. With no sight reference points over deep water, anglers are using loran (LOng RAnge Navigation) and GPS (Global Positioning System) to pinpoint specific areas that may hold active fish.

Depthfinders

The use of a flasher, which offers constant depth monitoring, convenience and portability is a modest beginning for today's electronic fisherman. Although easy to read, flashers barely tap the potential of electronics for increasing an angler's ability to "see" underwater.

The basis for these developments is sonar (SOund NAvigation Ranging), developed by the military during World War II for locating enemy submarines. The concept is a simple one: The main unit sends an electrical impulse through a transducer that is mounted somewhere on the boat. The transducer changes those electrical impulses to symmetrical, ever-widening sound waves that travel through the water.

A good sonar unit is a Great Lakes fisherman's best friend, as indicated by this nice salmon. Sophisticated depthfinders are a necessity in covering waters as large and diverse as the Great Lakes.

Salmon Gear—Electronic Aids

Whatever material those sound waves encounter—structure, fish, weeds, bottom—the message is sent back up to the transducer, converted back to electrical impulses and displayed on a paper graph or screen. The standard graph, paper-drive chart recorders or the more modern liquid crystal displays (LCD) or videos serve a useful purpose in locating fish or establishing fishing patterns.

"Because of the size and depth of the Great Lakes and similar bodies of water," said Mark McQuown, a representative of a depthfinding electronics firm, "the use of electronics has become an integral ingredient to success in locating fish ... and staying on them once you've found them."

Low-end LCDs were designed to provide information that the flasher doesn't. As the representative said, "Not only can you get a visual display to actually see what's going on in the world beneath you, but you can also pick up other important information, such as trolling speed and surface temperature—all on digital readout." The best part, he says, is that the price can be under $150 to purchase one of these units.

Two other areas of improvement to help meet the needs of fishermen are in screen quality and increased hands-off operation. Display screen visibility on some units actually improves in bright sunlight. In other words, the brighter the sun, the better you see the images on the screen. And, with improvements in signal processing, it's even easier to run an LCD unit. Some units incorporate automatic functions that analyze return echoes, adjust for interference problems internally, and provide an accurate read-out without the operator having to make adjustments.

As you move up the price ladder, mid- to high-priced units offer higher power for better depth penetration and higher resolution for an even clearer picture of the world beneath the boat. They also offer more bells and whistles, providing more information that you can adapt to your fishing approach.

Multi-functional units, a brainchild of advanced microchip technology, have made things easier for the consumer. Now, an angler can learn to operate one unit and have everything necessary for a successful fishing trip. At the same time, these units save much-needed space within the boat. Combination units for sonar, Loran-C and plotter (which may also include

More sophisticated depthfinders also have conservation and law enforcement applications. Here, Michigan conservation and tribal enforcement officers study graph paper showing illegal nets in use, in an area of Lake Michigan.

speed and surface temperature) range from under $500 to over $1,500.

While the low-end LCD's were supposed to replace flashers, the high-end LCDs were supposed to replace paper graphs. Don't expect a low-end unit to do the job of a paper graph or a high-end LCD.

With electronic units such as these, anglers are able to increase their proficiency on the water by reading what's going on below them and the boat's location in relation to structure, fish and baits being used.

A good example of utilizing a depthfinder to fine-tune your fishing approach is combining a graph with a 45-degree transducer off the back of the boat. This allows you to track the downrigger balls below your boat and determine where they are in relation to the fish, bait and/or thermocline.

Once the underwater "eyes" are working properly, the angler needs to acquire knowledge through experience to improve his success ratio. For example, if the lures off the downrigger balls are running below the fish being marked on the screen, they should be raised so that they're in or just above the fish zone. Fish will come up for a lure, but rarely will they go down to take a bait.

Another example involves the fish's reaction to the bait. If fish are seen streaking down from the downrigger set, there's probably something wrong. The boat may be going too fast, causing the lures to spin and spook the fish. The lures may be too close to the downrigger balls. Or, there might be a small fish on that wasn't big enough to trip the lure's release.

This is not knowledge you'll acquire overnight. The more time you spend on the water, the easier it'll be to interpret the information your equipment provides.

Personal preference also determines whether or not a paper graph is better suited for your needs than an LCD. Graphs provide an explicit and detailed picture of the world underneath the boat. You also have a record of your fishing efforts at the end of a roll of paper. However, LCDs do not run out of paper at the worst possible time, and you save the cost of the replacement paper. In many respects, LCDs are easier to operate.

The advancement of electronics technology in just a few short years has been remarkable. Some multi-functional units now bring together sonar, Loran-C and a plotter, as well as speed and surface temperature measuring devices—all in one box. With all that information at your fingertips, you can't help but be a better fisherman.

Loran-C

The Loran-C navigational aid can be used to increase an NAFC member's fishing success ratio, and to guide the angler safely back home. This electronic system leads navigators and anglers to within 50 to 100 feet of the intended water area.

Loran signals broadcast from many land-based stations. With signals from the main master station, plus two secondary stations, a boater can return to a predetermined spot through a

Plotting locations using a loran unit will make it easier to return to the exact location where fish were found. For successfully covering bodies of water like the Great Lakes, a loran unit is almost necessary.

process of triangulation. Reference charts should then be used to determine precise geographic location; such maps are available from your U.S. Army Corps of Engineers office.

As an example of its use, charter captain Del Rowles was trolling over 500 feet of water when the Olcott, New York, skipper started to mark a large baitfish school. As he trolled through the area, he had a release on one of his downriggers. He immediately plugged this spot into his Loran-C, and worked the area several times with downriggers and Dipsy Divers.

"Once you locate a school of active fish," says Rowles, "it's important to be able to stay on them. Loran allows you to do that more effectively than anything I know. If I didn't have it on my boat, we may have never done as well as we did. It also serves as a most useful navigational aid should the lake flip over

Salmon Depths

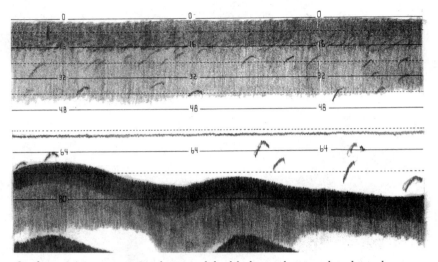

On this artist's representation of an actual depthfinder graph paper, the salmon show up as inverted v's. This results from the change in distance of the sonar's signal as the cone crosses over the fish.

and we encounter a fog bank. It's great just for finding my way back home after a long day of fishing. The more direct route saves me time and gas, which means more money in my pocket."

Some Loran-C units have a built-in plotter to show you the course you're running, and where you are catching fish. You can repeat your successful trolling angles much more rapidly, identifying where you've been, and what you need to do to get back on that course. The plotter complements the Loran-C, and presents a visual picture of the loran information. For some, reading a picture is easier than reading numbers and trying to relate these numbers to a chart.

The fishing public can now have quality electronics at a relatively nominal cost. With the upsurge in technology, Loran-C units now are one-tenth the cost of early models. With this kind of pricing, the average fisherman can afford having these navigational aids on board. In fact, he can't afford *not* to.

Global Positioning System

The Navstar Global Positioning System (GPS), a new

navigational system, operates off signals from 23 orbital satellites. The major advantage to this type of navigational aid is that the signals travel a more direct path from outer space, instead of from land-based transmitters. As a result, there will be fewer interference problems from mountains, trees, buildings or other such land obstructions. In some areas of the country, Loran-C can't be used because of this type of interference. GPS will open these areas up to boaters in search of navigational aids. Because of the more direct signal, GPS also is slightly more accurate. The biggest advantage for fishermen, however, is the fewer interference problems. However, this is still new technology, so GPS units are relatively expensive, but prices are dropping drastically as manufacturers compete for market share.

Although 24-hour satellite coverage is already in place, you needn't get rid of the Loran-C unit just yet. While these units still meet the needs of the angling public, the government will continue to operate the transmitter towers needed for Loran-C. The choice is up to you.

Other types of electronic aids available to today's anglers include:

• Marine radios which are essential when deep-water trolling for safety and basic communication purposes. You can report emergencies on the U.S. Coast Guard emergency broadcast channel (16), or receive updated radio reports on the weather. You can also talk to fellow anglers to get fishing updates from around the area.

• State-of-the-art monitoring devices that can measure water clarity, pH, speed and water temperature both on the surface and at the downrigger ball. Individual units are also available that will give you a reading of both speed and temperature at your downrigger ball, which may vary considerably with surface temperature and speed.

7

Salmon Gear—Ideal Boats

B oats are an integral part of today's salmon fishing scene. Although shore-fishing options are available, the use of on-water vessels greatly enhances an angler's ability to chase salmon, and extends one's season considerably. Choosing one boat over another, though, becomes a matter of personal preference, and whether it meets your needs. Personal fishing style comes into play, as does the size of the body of water that it will be used upon. You should select a boat that meets established requirements, from Great Lakes downrigger trolling to river drift fishing. It's not an easy choice, and you must make your selection carefully.

Even identifying specific needs in some cases does little to narrow your selection. For example, if you needed to select a Great Lakes trolling vessel, the list of choices would be a long one. Is it suited for rough water? Deep water trolling? Is it maneuverable? What about: Size—how many people will it hold? A cabin? Soft or hard top (if any)? Hull design? Will it be used for pleasure fishing or for charter fishing? What size and type motor is needed? How important is fuel efficiency? Is trailering ability a factor? Should it be fiberglass or aluminum? All these questions need to be answered, and it isn't an easy decision. Boats differ as much as the people purchasing them.

A charter captain, for example, prefers a straight inboard, sporting a big porch area for the fishing comfort of his clients. For him, it also should offer a shelter area to keep people out of

It's important to select a boat that best fits your needs. River drift fishing, like this, is usually done from a 16- to 18-foot deep-v aluminum boat because it's easier to control in current and when fighting fish. Larger boats are better for deep-water trolling on large lakes.

Salmon Gear—Ideal Boats

the elements, and maintain a low profile in the water, with a high upswept bow to handle rough weather.

The same type of analysis is needed for a river-fishing boat. Whether it's a MacKenzie River-type drift boat or a standard deep-v, 16- or 18-foot aluminum, assess your wants and needs in a fishing boat, and then look for the craft that best meets them.

If you're looking for a larger boat and you've got a general idea of what you want, you should be able to find a charter boat that is similar, or even identical, to what you're looking for that you can hire or ask questions about.

Even if you're not sure what you need, charter skippers are a good place to start. Local marina operators can be extremely helpful, especially if there's potential for a sale.

One of the best ways to determine what you're looking for in a boat, though, is to join a fishing organization that best exemplifies your fishing style. Get to know the members who are usually willing to share expertise and knowledge about boats and fishing. It's a great way to learn, and you'll make new angling buddies in the process.

For those who don't want to invest in a boat for big waters, there are the charter boats. Charter fishing and guide services have become more and more competitive and popular in today's fishing market, especially in the Great Lakes Basin.

Whatever the reason for chartering a fishing trip, the experience itself should be worth the effort and expense. Boats are better equipped; captains more knowledgeable, and services more convenient. Here are some tips on making that important, charter service selection:

• Don't be afraid to ask questions regarding the service you're considering. Find out all you can about the captain, and the services offered. For instance, does he or she offer free fish-cleaning after the trip?

• Find out what sponsors support a particular service. For example, if the captain is a Pro Staffer for Lowrance or Big Jon Downriggers, you know those manufacturers feel comfortable being represented by him.

• Ask for references and follow up by calling one or two of them. Would they charter with that captain again? What was the catch? Although catches will vary by day and season, see if they match the picture painted by the captain.

• Never shop by price alone. In most instances, you get what you pay for. Inquire as to boat size. How long has the captain been chartering in these waters? Is he full or part-time? Remember a full-time captain is someone who's in the business to make a living. He's on the water nearly every day, so he's familiar with current conditions. This is especially important when fishing turns slow because of the weather. How many charters did the service run last year?

• Be wary of gimmicks. There's no "guarantee" out there on the water, and there's usually something behind those "discounted" packages. Most charters need to get a specified amount of money for each charter to cover costs of dockage, gas, mate, equipment and the like. Discounts normally don't fit into the picture.

• Other questions to ask: Do they run a first mate? Make sure they do, for both fishing pleasure and safety. How long are your trips? Are they from dock to dock? How do they handle deposits? Do they help make rooming arrangements? What happens in case of inclement weather? How far do they make a run (on the average) before fishing? What kind of catch is typical for that time of year?

• The bottom line is that this should be the fishing experience that you'll remember for a lifetime. Captains rely on repeat business, so your trip should be an enjoyable one— whether you catch a mess of fish or not. Catch numbers should not weigh that heavily in your decision to return, however. You can tell when you've had a good time with someone—how sincere they are and how hard they fished for you.

And, just like the fishing, there is no guarantee that you'll end up having the best fishing trip you've ever dreamed of. However, by taking the time to ask questions, you can greatly increase your chances of finding just the right captain and service to meet your needs.

8

Shallow Trolling Gear

ishermen are forever tinkering with gadgets and gear that might more easily take hooks down to salmon, attract them better or trick the fish more effectively. Of the hundreds of new items devised each year, some truly well-thought-out accessories have endured to become versatile fishing tools every salmon angler should consider taking on fishing trips.

Let's arbitrarily divide a wide range of salmon fishing depth-seeking devices into two overlapping categories: Items that aid an angler to take salmon from the surface to about 80 feet deep, and other gear that fishes best from 50 to more than 200 feet deep.

The shallow-range fishing equipment includes divers, paravanes, outriggers, planers and trolling boards. Plumbing the depths can be best accomplished using downriggers, drop weights, lead-core lines and wire-line fishing gear.

Divers

Most divers are hand-sized, and salmon fishermen generally carry several color options of their favorite make of diver—pink, fire orange or chartreuse—in either standard or fluorescent finishes. Carrying two to three sizes of these divers offers a choice of depths to which they will take terminal rigs. A small diver may, depending on the weight of line used, best scourge salmon schools at 10 to 40 feet, the mid-size model sinks

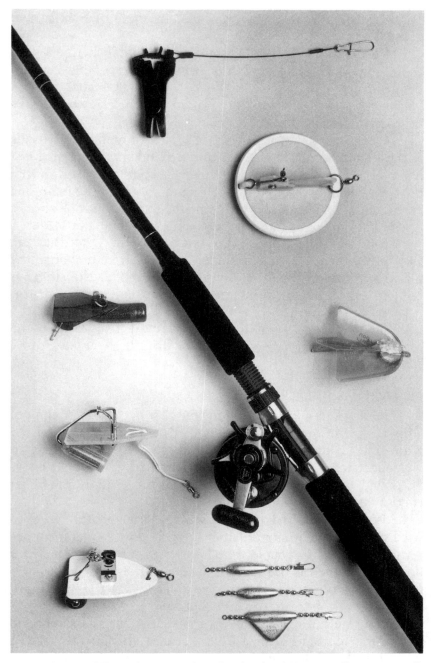

Divers take some different shapes, as indicated in this photo. However, all serve essentially the same purpose for shallow trolling. Also shown are a release clip for use off of a downrigger (top) and three versions of popular trolling weights.

Shallow Trolling Gear

50 to 80 feet and the largest size can go to more than twice that depth.

The divers' well-chosen names captivate fishermen with their suggestions of mysterious or seductive happenings beneath the surface. "Deep Six," "Pink Lady," "Oregon Diver," "Dancer," "Dipsy" and "Jet Planer" monickers sound like fish-catching aids, and they are.

Divers have a flat, thin body of plastic or metal that is wide at the squared-off front and narrow or rounded at the rear. Most have a raised tower, heavy wire superstructure or lever arm that provides a sliding or unpinning attachment where the main line connects. Lead weights at the front (generally, but not always, at the bottom) of each diver help achieve a diving attitude.

The Jet Planer does not trip, but has a lead sinker that can slide a few inches on a wire under its body to help change the planer's attitude. When in diving-fishing mode, the sinker is held by gravity at the front or downward end of the device. After a strike, the planer's rear end cocks downward and the lead sinker slides several inches toward the rear to hold the planer at an upward tilt which helps bring the salmon to the surface.

Depth Is Limited

There are physical limitations on how deep a diver can go. This is determined by the amount of planing surface and the main-line diameter. Large-diameter monofilament, such as 30-pound test, will not carry an identical diver as deep as 12-pound line, because of increased surface tension and water friction around the line.

Also, there is a maximum depth that can be attained even with small-diameter monofilament, reached when water surface tension around a couple hundred yards of line overcomes downward force on the planing face and the diver will go no deeper. As more line is let out, the diver rises as the line begins to bow upward from its lowest point.

Main line ties to a swivel on the sliding bar or locking and unpinning mechanism of a diver. Leader and lure go on the trailing end. When lowered into the water, your boat's forward motion causes the diver to bite down into the water.

Some listed devices also can be adjusted to run to left or

NAFC Member Herman Bushman took this 16-pound coho in 40 feet of Lake Ontario's water. He used 15-pound-test line with a Dipsy Diver, dodger and shrimp combination. It was caught in early August.

right as well as down, so that they will swing out to either side of the boat's path, enticing salmon wary of shadows or motor noise. Manufacturers' diver packages generally contain a helpful table of depths showing how deep each size trolling aid will go with different diameters of line.

Color, reflections of light off the planing surfaces and inviting wriggles draw salmon to divers and the artificial lures or bait trailing them. On a strike, the unpinning mechanism pops free or the sliding swivel moves to the front of its travel bar, changing the attitude of divers to an upward-planing position.

Some of the divers have adjusting screws to change the amount of force required to trip them. This prevents light taps, missed strikes or weight of weeds snagged by lure or hooks from prematurely triggering the diver into its upward mode, thus eliminating constant reeling-in to reset the diver.

To remove a "shaker" (small fish) betrayed by spasmodic twitching of your rodtip, or to bring a diver in to clean off weeds and inspect the lure, is fairly simple. Raise your rodtip high and then quickly lower the tip, throwing slack into your line. Come back sharply and strongly on the rod and you should

Shallow Trolling Gear

This nice king was taken on a Dipsy Diver and spoon combination. The diver was pinned with a Jettison release that allowed the angler to use a longer lead.

trip the diver's mechanism into its upward mode.

One drawback to fishing with divers is that weeds can slide down the line to the diver's unpinning device, wedging it in the downward mode. When this happens, the easiest way to bring it in is to slow or stop your boat's travel so you can crank in line without adding forward-movement pressure.

Paravanes

Close relatives of divers are paravanes which rely on long, tapering fins at each side of their bodies and a front weight to achieve depth. One popular model conceals both its weight and a snubber inside its bulbous body. Another paravane looks like an upside-down paper airplane that school children learn to fold. This model allows adjustment for different depths by attaching the main line to one of several holes in the upper of its three fins, and also permits left-right travel control by attaching your leader to a choice of drilled holes in trailing edges of the other two fins.

Paravanes do not trip. The weight of a salmon on the leader behind the paravane will, though, neutralize it so it won't affect the act of reeling fish to the boat. Lures and baits fished behind paravanes can be checked periodically by letting your outboard idle while the lines to be checked are reeled in.

Outrigger Poles

Outrigger poles, also called "wings," are used to fish lines parallel to, but well away from, the stern lines. They can separate lines when you're trolling with more than three or four rods. Also, outrigger poles widen the area which can be covered during one trolling pass and often can generate more strikes than stern lines because the outrigger lines are away from the boat's shadow and motor wake.

The outrigger poles generally are from 12 to 18 feet long and mounted at 90 degrees to the boat's centerline. Most are one-piece, but longer outrigger rods can be two-piece. An endless loop of cord and a pulley system is used to carry fishing lines to the tips of outrigger rods.

Because of the number of lines, it is necessary to make slow, sweeping turns when changing or reversing course, to prevent tangling the lines. That's the bad news. The good news is salmon often take a lure or bait on such a turn. What happens is rigs on the outside of the turn will move faster and rise, while enticers on the inside of the turn slow down and sink. One or the other action might appeal to a salmon trailing the lure, but the fish does not bite until there is a change in action or speed. Much the same thing occurs when a boat with stern lines only makes "S" curves.

Here's how this works: A line-release mechanism is attached to the pulley line; the fisherman's reel is left in free spool under thumb control, and 40 to 120 feet of line are let out. Then, the line clips into the release mechanism and the release goes out by hand on the pulley cord to the outrigger rodtip. The reel then drops into gear, and the rod butt is set into a holder. When a salmon strikes, the release pops, freeing the main line.

To reload, hand-haul pulley line back to the starting position and again attach the angling line to its release mechanism.

Flashers And Dodgers

Bright, brash and noisy, flashers and dodgers have greatly aided salmon trollers in attracting fish to their hooks. They have been used on the West Coast since 1932, when tackle maker Les Davis sold the first models of these bent, metal pieces. Now, flashers and dodgers come in sizes ranging from 4 inches long and 1 to 1½ inches wide to blades 14 inches long and 4 inches wide. You can buy these attractors in either metal or plastic and each can be decked-out with reflective tape panels enhancing their effectiveness.

Today's flashers and dodgers are readily used from inshore waters, lakes and reservoirs of the West Coast through the big impoundments of the Dakotas to the Great Lakes. They have helped boost salmon catches wherever used because of three things they add to presentation of trolled lures or baits.

Vibrations, caused by passage of these attractors through the water, draw salmon toward the source. Reflections from the metal blades or tape panels and the bright colors of some plastic flashers and dodgers make them highly visible to fish. The attractors impart lively, swimming action to lures or baits fished behind them.

Flashers and dodgers are not identical in appearance, require different rigging, and seldom are fished simultaneously because each works best at different trolling speeds. Flashers are trolled at a faster pace than are dodgers.

Flashers are narrower than dodgers in proportion to their length and sharply bent up on one end and down on the other relatively squared-off end. They are designed to rotate 360 degrees. Dodgers generally are shorter and a bit wider in relation to length than flashers. Dodgers also are flat but have well-rounded ends with slightly curved lips—again, facing in opposite directions. They are designed to be fished at a slower trolling speed which causes them to wigwag from side to side.

Rotating flashers create the illusion of "live" action in lures that have very little swimming ability of their own, such as squid, hoochies, bucktails and flies. They enhance the presentation of whole herring, anchovies or smelt by giving them

The Abe & Al No. 2 Flasher (top) is designed to rotate when it's trolled while the No. 1 Herring Dodger (bottom) is intended to wag from side to side. Trolling speed is critical to the proper operation of each.

the "shake, rattle and roll" of darting, frantic baitfish.

Every salmon angler settles upon a favorite length of leader to use with flashers. However, an average leader generally measures about 1½ to 2½ times the flasher's length. After attaching leader and bait or lure, lower the flasher into the water from a boat which is slowly moving. Then, motor speed is gradually increased until the flasher begins to rotate fully. Do not throttle up past this point, because the flasher might then whip your lure or bait too fast for a salmon to grab.

A flasher that misses one beat in about 12 to 15 turns is fine-tuned to near perfection. Line is then let out from the angler's reel for the desired distance from the boat and attached to a downrigger or Jet Diver. Then, the rod is inserted into a rod holder on the rail or transom. When a salmon strikes, it's

Shallow Trolling Gear

generally solidly hooked.

Dodgers are commonly used with lures or baits that have built-in action of their own, but these attractors are effective with any lure. Leader length can be varied so that bait, squid, hoochies, trolling spoons or plugs are trolled with imparted lifelike action. Leader lengths used with dodgers will range from 10 to 18 inches for bait, squid and hoochies to as much as 2½ or 3 feet for trolling spoons or plugs. Usually, however, the leaders are about 1¼ to 1½ times the dodger's length.

As with flashers, the rigged dodger and bait or lure are lowered into the water so you can watch the action and motor speed is adjusted until the dodger wags seductively. If it begins to spin, back off on the throttle until side-to-side motion is resumed and constant.

Leader Twist And Swivels

The biggest bugaboo in trolling with flashers or dodgers is leader twist, because it destroys the effective presentation of lure or bait. Leader twist can be caused by letting out your main line and gear too quickly, making sharp turns with the boat, or catching weeds or grass on the hook. Twist can be partly prevented by carefully and slowly feeding terminal gear into the water, making only slow, wide turns, and maintaining proper trolling speed. Adding a high-quality, ball-bearing swivel between attractor blade and leader helps, too.

Your selection of monofilament also determines whether you will be plagued by leader twist. Using a stiff, less flexible line and leader will result in less untangling and retying than if you use a more flexible mono. Preventing twists allows you more fishing time.

Weed And Grass Check

An experienced salmon troller will watch his rodtip's pulsations while fishing with flasher or dodger gear. There's the steady "beat-beat-beat" of efficiently working equipment. Erratic twitches may mean a small fish has taken the hook and is being towed along. Lack of a pulsating beat might mean your equipment has been fouled by weeds, jellyfish or grass. Salmon will seldom grab a fouled bait or lure.

Trolling gear should be reeled in every 20 to 30 minutes for

This handsome, 25½-pound chinook salmon fell victim to NAFC Charter Member Tom Pouttu's offering. Pouttu was trolling aboard a South Eastern Charter's boat on Lake Huron, off Grindstone City, Michigan.

Shallow Trolling Gear

a line and leader check. Clean, natural looking baits and lures will catch more salmon. If you're using bait, examine the body of the baitfish for tooth marks, scrapes or missing scales indicating that the bait has been "taste tested." If it has been, you should make a second pass through the same area.

Snubbers

Any salmon can belt a trolled bait or lure with awesome speed and force. Big salmon have slammed fishing gear hard enough to break rods and strip gears on reels. For this reason, most salmon fishermen set reel drags carefully to absorb a fish's strike. They also release line for the first run or two so the gear isn't stressed to the breaking point.

An accessory called a "snubber" helps cushion vicious strikes and can blunt the powerful lunges of a wall-mount-sized salmon. The snubber is a length of surgical tubing with a barrel swivel on each end and heavy shock line, longer than the snubber, inside the tubing, connecting the two swivels.

The tubing will stretch inches before the shock line comes into play. This snubber may be most functional behind a flasher or dodger, but many anglers prefer to install it ahead of the attractor blade in the belief that if it's farther from the bait, salmon will be less likely to see it and shy from it.

Planer Boards/In-Line Side Planers

Planer boards, although relatively new in sportfishing, gained in popularity on the Great Lakes during the 1980s. The boards were an instant success with trolling techniques applied to salmon and trout, and later were adapted to other freshwater fish species throughout the basin—especially for walleye.

Planer boards added a whole new dimension to fishing strategies. Smaller trolling vessels were able to compete with bigger boats because they could cover more area in a shorter period of time. Overall fishing effectiveness increased in a number of ways, many of which will be discussed here. Some people, considered experts in the field of fishing, believe that fishing efficiency can be increased by as much as 90 percent when using a "down and out" planer-board system.

A planer board is nothing more than a device that allows you to spread your lure presentation away from either side of the

Using planer boards, as this angler is doing, provides the benefit of covering more water in one pass. It also presents bait where boat noise won't spook the target.

Shallow Trolling Gear

boat. The boards can be constructed of wood, metal or polyurethane. Some sort of ballast is needed to keep the boards upright.

Installation depends upon the type of boat you're outfitting. If you've got easy access to the bow, a bow-mount boom (mast) will suffice. If not, you'll want to use a double-mast system, rigged for either side of the boat. This system normally is used on bigger boats, in the 26-foot-and-larger range. Operators of bigger boats, when selecting a mast system, should also consider using a recoil system to help compensate for boat movement. If there's no recoil system, some form of rubber snubber may be needed to absorb any stressful shock associated with operating the boat in rough water.

Ideally, the boom or mast can be secured with the backer plate underneath the deck or gunwale with good, solid stainless steel nuts and bolts. However, if there's no way to use a backer plate, use a well nut to secure the boom/mast. Simply drill a hole the size of a well nut and insert the nut into it. As you screw the unit into the nut, the well nut expands to lock it into place. Use a well nut with a fiber insert. With the insert, the nut acts as a lock washer. Installation is normally easy, and you can be up and running in no time at all.

Placement of the rod holders can be as critical as the boom itself. The holders need to be attached where they can be easily reached, and properly spaced for sufficient separation of reels and rodtips to avoid tangles.

With the boom/mast and holders in place, you're ready to start trolling. Place your planer boards into the water and start to let out your towline, which usually is a high-visibility, braided dacron line. This line is strong, very visible for "strike" watching and can be seen better by other boaters. Show as much courtesy as possible toward your fellow boaters. Planer boards are an extension of your boat, and they're your responsibility. Most planer-board manufacturers use high-visibility colors on the boards, as well as courtesy tracking flags to make the boards more visible. If you're making your own boards (How-to-build instructions periodically appear in major fishing magazines.), be sure to take color into consideration. Again, they're your responsibility.

The boat's forward motion combined with the planer board's design makes the device track away from the boat to the

end of the towline. The more line you release, the farther the board will track to the side of your vessel. This distance usually will vary depending upon personal preference, nearby boat traffic and weather conditions.

Fishermen using the planer board for the first time should rig whatever is convenient for the boat, and operate only one side until they become familiar with how the boards work and what they'll do when trolling. Study it all, and then move on to using both sides.

Lure selection for planer-board fishing depends upon seasonal migration patterns for salmon. For example, spring fishing may dictate small stickbaits. You may want to experiment with shallow and deep-diving plugs to determine the fish's preferences for that day. Either way, your daily patterns and presentations are limited only by your imagination.

Once you select a lure, make sure it's tracking properly for the speed at which you're trolling. Then, you'll want to start letting line out for the lead you'll be attaching to the towline. Remember, keep everything consistent, and work in a symmetrical pattern, so you can avoid tangles when a fish strikes.

Leads also will vary with the season. Springtime trolling may command 50- to 150-foot leads, depending on the weather and water depth. Water clarity can be another factor. Leads should be long enough allowing you to catch fish, but not too long. With longer leads, you lose hook-setting power because of the stretch in the line.

With the length of lead determined, clip a planer board release to the fishing line. Then, connect this to the towline, being sure to allow for free movement along the towline. As you peel line from the reel, the boat's movement and the lure's resistance in the water will pull your lure and line farther out. Your outside line should be within 2 to 4 feet of the board. Place that rod in its holder, and set up your second rod in the same manner, stopping its towline connection 3 to 5 feet from the first line. This allows enough space between the two lines for lure travel and boat turning.

With a set pattern or methodology established, you can see that this type of fishing can be effective in many ways:

• Planer boards can help you get in tight to shore when early-season action in warm water pockets dictates a shallow presentation. Also, when fishing shallower depths, or when fish suspend near the surface, planer boards will help you take fish that may have been spooked by the boat noise, and, of course, help you pick up fish that are far enough from the boat to be unaware of its presence.

• Charter boat captain Jeremiah Heffernan of North Tonawanda, New York, is an excellent example of someone using imagination to adapt different ideas to planer-board fishing. In an effort to establish a controlled-depth fishing pattern in deeper water, he has combined jet planers with the boards to hit a predetermined depth which is a prime target zone for fish because of the water temperature at that depth. He may also vary the depths he's covering with the lures to blanket more water—and, ultimately, catch more fish.

• Joe Prince, with Prince Mastercraft, has had similar ideas for increasing fishing success. He has used drop weights or other types of divers, such as Dipsy Divers. He has run 1-pound drop weights off planer boards as deep as 100 feet, and used ½-pound weights as deep as 40 to 60 feet. Another of his favorites is to run a three-way swivel, with a deep-diving crankbait off the bottom, and a lighter spoon off the trailing eye. If you need to go deeper, add weight to the line, either with a jettison release or with a keel sinker-swivel combination.

His tip, for protecting the environment, is to use pre-rigged, concrete weights in place of the lead drop balls that are commonly used. Again, use your imagination.

"Anyone fishing the Great Lakes for salmon should at least go with a double set of planer boards," says Prince. "A double set of planer boards is more effective because offshore winds will have a tendency to push you around quite a bit."

Triple boards are also available, designed for the Great Lakes with a shorter chop (like Lake Erie) or to compensate for the additional buoyancy when running several divers or heavy drop weights off to one side of the boat. Lead-core line can also be run off boards.

Now that you know the basic concept of planer-board fishing, do some research before you buy. Because you'll usually get what you pay for, don't go bargain hunting. Ask the manufacturers for comparison information, and why their unit is better. If you have any questions on rigging up your own

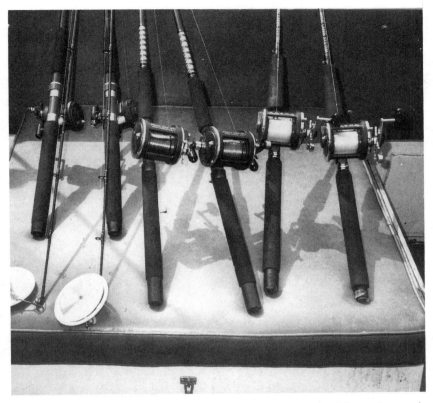

Diving planes have proven to be an effective addition to the Great Lakes fisherman's arsenal. As shown here, these divers are used along with downrigger equipment to give additional depth control.

system or any fishing techniques already mentioned, don't be afraid to ask the manufacturers, either. Planer boards are here to stay, so hop on the bandwagon and learn the finer points of Great Lakes trolling. You won't be sorry.

The same basic principles of planer-board use apply to in-line side planers, but on a much smaller scale. In fact, it's on a one-to-one basis between rod and side planer. As a result, it's much less expensive. More importantly, in-line planers can be every bit as effective.

In-line boards also incorporate the use of a release to secure the board after an established lead has been set. One of two ways can be used while trolling.

The most popular way is setting the release so that the planer slides freely down the line after the fish hits (unlike

Dipsy Diver Design

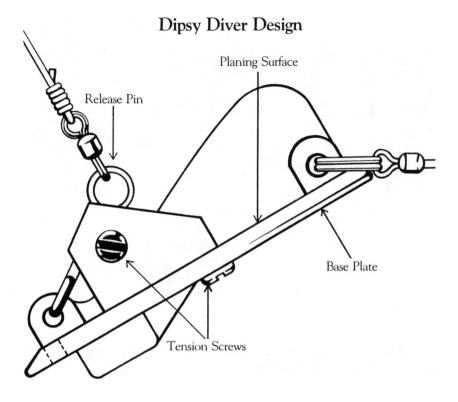

Release Pin

Planing Surface

Base Plate

Tension Screws

This diagram shows the elements of a popular diving plane, or trolling/diving sinker. A snap-on "O" ring that increases the planing surface (and diving capabilities) is available and easy to install.

planer boards where the line is disengaged from the system after a fish hits). By placing a split shot a few feet above the lure, the device will stop short of the lure.

A second way is tightening the release so the in-line board also serves as a strike indicator for any size fish. Then, when there is a strike, you'll need to reel the device in and remove it in order to fight the fish freely. Be careful, though, that you *don't* allow any slack line during this process or it could mean lost fish.

These pocket-size planers offer advantages over the bigger boards. For example, trolling can be done at slower speeds (under 1.5 mph) because a towline isn't being used. Releases on in-line planers can still occur even at slower, live-bait trolling speeds. And, you have as many terminal tackle-rigging options with this smaller, yet extremely versatile, trolling tool.

Captain Steve Robards, who operates out of St. Joseph's, Michigan, and divides his time between Lakes Michigan and Ontario for salmon, has added the in-line planer to his daily routine. Cohos and kings are both excellent targets from spring until fall with this method. Running planer-to-bait leads of 30 to 80 feet, he adds weight 3 to 4 feet in front of the bait (⅛ ounce, ¼ ounce or ¾ ounce—depending on where fish are holding) to target salmon that are traditionally deeper.

His favorite bait, which he runs 95 percent of the time, is the trolling spoon. He'll use small- or large-sized spoons to match the size of baitfish in the area he's fishing. When running in-line planers, he'll use his regular downrigger rods or heavier rods normally used with diver planers to compensate for the additional tension. He normally runs 15- to 20-pound-test line.

One disadvantage to the in-line planers is controlling them in rough water. With large waves, you'll need to keep them closer to the boat to keep them under control. And, as with their larger cousins, it's your responsibility to keep them out of the paths of other trollers.

In-line planers also can be used quite effectively for salmon in rivers, because the current pulls your line out away from the shoreline. Thus, you can fish like a boater, without a boat. No longer does the angler have to rely strictly on drift tackle. It opens a whole new realm of possibilities for the shore-bound fisherman. As is true with fishing in general, your options are only limited by your imagination.

9

Deep Trolling Gear

Perhaps no single innovation has made as much of an impact in the world of Great Lakes salmon fishing as the downrigger. As a result of that success, downrigger use has affected a wide range of species and waters from coast to coast where controlled-depth fishing translates into increased success.

Electronics can show you where the fish are located, but if you can't get your lures or baits into the specific depth zone where the fish will strike, you're not going to produce consistently on the water.

Simply put, a downrigger allows you to place a heavy weight at a specific depth beneath the boat. Your fishing line attaches to a special release on the downrigger weight, or is stacked on the cable itself. When a fish hits, the line pulls from the release, and a happy angler fights the fish with only rod, reel and line—no heavy weight to contend with. After the fish has been boated, simply crank up the downrigger ball and do it all over again. Sound simple enough? Well, it is.

Whether it's the controlled-depth trolling for suspended salmon and trout, anchoring in rivers to let the current supply the necessary lure action while the downriggers keep the lure at the proper depth, or dragging the downrigger weights on the bottom to stir up inactive fish, the downrigger can work wonders for you no matter where, or what quarry you might be attempting to boat.

Complete Angler's Library

Downriggers are virtually standard equipment on vessels trolling the Great Lakes. The depth control downriggers provide for deep trolling results in more consistent fishing success.

Deep Trolling Gear

Boat size doesn't matter. Downriggers work on small or large boats. Larger boats, though, have more space so operators can put together specialized "programs," creating a set simulating a baitfish school, for example.

Downriggers in the back of the boat, extending out to the sides (port and starboard) are referred to as outside downriggers or "out-downs." Depending on the beam of the boat, and the pattern you intend to fish, corner downriggers can be placed, as well as one or two center downriggers. With five 'riggers, you're able to run patterns in the shape of a "W," "M" and "V." With six downriggers, add a "U" to the aforementioned options. Leads off the downriggers are important to maintain consistency.

With downriggers, you can get as simple or as sophisticated as you want. There are portable mounts that attach to the side of your boat or railing; gimbal mounts that fit nicely in rod holders; wood or aluminum mounting boards on the boat's stern that can handle downrigger mounting in quantity, or stationary base or swivel-base mounts that attach directly to the boat.

How well downriggers work is directly related to the operator. Try to envision what's going on beneath your boat each time you place a lure with your downrigger. This will help you come up with a visual pattern or picture of the baitfish school you're trying to simulate for the kind of fish you're targeting.

As mentioned earlier, lead lengths are extremely important in downrigger fishing, especially when targeting salmon. While springtime fishing for salmon in cold, shallow, clear waters, you'll want to go with longer leads. Fishing in deeper, murky water calls for shorter leads.

"Run your leads just long enough to allow you to catch fish," says charter captain John Emory of Traverse City, Michigan. "Never run your leads longer than you have to. Not only do you lose hook-setting power from line stretch, but you also lose action on the lures you're using."

When putting together the downrigger set you hope to run, take into consideration other methods that will help you get more baits or lures into the water. For stacking lines on the same downrigger, a rubber band or some type of spring-action clip will hold the lure in place on the cable. It's another form of controlled-depth fishing because you know exactly where your lure or bait is. Or, you can work a free-floating slider rig off the

Sliders, Stackers On Downriggers

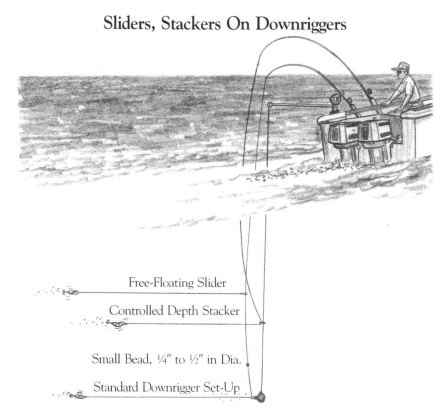

Free-Floating Slider

Controlled Depth Stacker

Small Bead, ¼″ to ½″ in Dia.

Standard Downrigger Set-Up

Sliders or stackers help you get more lures into the water at different depths without having to use additional rods. The stacked lure naturally runs about halfway down the line because of the line's bow caused by trolling.

same downrigger rod by placing a snap swivel at either end of a 4- to 5-foot piece of monofilament line. Attach a lure at one end and the main fishing line to the other. You're now running two different baits off one rod.

A free-floating slider will never run below the middle of the natural bow that's formed in the line when it's trolled through the water. If you set your downrigger for 50 feet, look for your slider to be roughly 25 feet down. Because it floats free, you have to react quickly when you have a hit. Reel down as quickly as possible. Once you feel tension, make a quick hookset.

Here's a little trick to prevent losing a choice salmon during a battle when there's a slider on the line: Put a colored bead (up to ½-inch in diameter) just above the snap swivel of the main line from the rod. When a fish hits the bait on a free-floating slider, the increased tension on the line brings the two swivels together and they can work against each other to open up, especially when it's a feisty Great Lakes salmon. The bead serves as a spacer to keep the swivels apart, and also as an attractant for the lure.

Charter captain Pete Ruboyianes of Crown Point, Indiana, who works both Lake Michigan and Lake Ontario, used the free-floating slider method during a Lake Ontario Pro-Am Salmon Team Tournament. After targeting a thermal pocket that was holding fish, he discovered the fish were ball-shy. So, he ran the downrigger balls below the pocket, and used sliders to place small spoons into the pocket. This resulted in a first-place finish for him in the tournament. One month later, he used a similar tactic to win a Lake Michigan tournament.

You need to experiment with different fish-catching methods. For example, off the downrigger, you can run a dodger down deep, and take advantage of its attractant qualities by stacking spoons or shallow-running stickbaits around it. Or, substitute other attractant devices.

Running a specific pattern such as an "M" or "W" can be very effective. Not only are you covering a wider area of water with little chance of tangling, but you can be targeting different fish species in different temperature zones at the same time.

Bait selection for use with downriggers is a mixed bag. Some prefer to use all the same spoons and colors. Others choose similar-type spoons or baits, but keep the same colors on each downrigger, including stackers and sliders. Still, others like to mix-and-match to see what the fish want for that particular day. To do this, they run a variety of baits. This isn't easy to do, especially when some baits are designed to work at specific (and different) speeds.

Get The Lead Out

Here's an ingenious way for salmon anglers to fish with many ounces of ball sinker weight, yet battle a hooked fish on bare, weight-free line. This is kind of like "having your cake and eating it too."

Tie a sinker release mechanism between main line and leader. A barrel swivel at one end of the mechanism is fixed,

Drop Sinker Rig

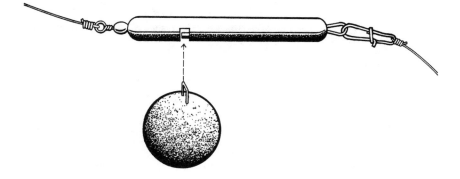

Salmon anglers—particularly those on the West Coast—use a drop sinker rig so they can battle salmon with a weightless line. A heavy sinker locks into a dropper mechanism which releases the weight when a salmon strikes.

but the opposite (rear) end of the release looks much like a sturdy cotter pin. This end enters the cylinder's center and locks through a short, tough spring inside the mechanism. Slip the eye of the ball weight into the release slot of the cylindrical tube, and you can fish with 8 to 48 ounces of depth-seeking lead until a salmon strikes. Then, the sinker drops away, leaving no added weight on your line while you concentrate on slugging it out with the salmon.

To load the sinker weight, pull on the leader end of the release cylinder and the spring-loaded pin slides past the slot opening to permit a sinker eye to enter the slot. Releasing the tension allows the pin to slide back, securely holding the sinker.

The spring tension normally takes a strong pull of about 4 pounds or more (some releases can be set higher) to release the weight, so shakers can be freed without sacrificing your lead. But, when the sinker drops off during a hefty strike, you know the salmon "pulling the pin" is a good one.

Lead Core: A Successful Compromise

Salmon anglers who dislike heavy sinkers and the added knots required to insert swivels or weight releases into their lines may choose to fish with lead-core lines. These take baits and lures to medium depths with smooth efficiency and maintain good control in the fishing zone.

Braided nylon sheathing covers a soft lead core. The nylon is color-coded in 25-foot or 10-yard increments, depending on the manufacturer. Thus, you know instantly how much line is out when a fish strikes. After landing that fish, the angler simply pays out the same number of colors, returning his tackle to the same depth and distance to tempt another fish.

A salmon fisherman has a choice of lead-core line tests from about 12 pounds to 45 pounds. Most lead-core line is sold in two connected spools of 100 yards each. An 18- to 35-foot monofilament leader, slightly lighter in breaking strength than the lead core, attaches to the lead-core line with a nail knot.

Large-capacity reels are required for lead-core line because of the line's large diameter. Lead core does not kink frequently and retains a high degree of flexibility, with little stretch. Given proper care, it can last indefinitely.

Wired For Action

Three types of wire line are available for salmon fishing, including Monel, stainless steel and braided wire. Each will give you extremely sensitive "feel" for the action of your terminal gear. Every wriggle of a plug and light tap of a nibbling salmon are telegraphed up the non-stretching line.

Spooling up with wire line is relatively inexpensive. However, a critical drawback to "fishing wire" is that each wire line will sooner or later acquire weakening kinks that can be disastrous when hooking or playing a big fish.

When the wire kinks, each lunge and pull of a salmon fatigues the metal (much like breaking a clothes hanger by bending it back and forth). It can pop at boatside when you're trying to drag a lunker to the net. To delay the onset of kinks, wire line users must unspool and retrieve smoothly. Also, the wire should be carefully checked for twists and kinks each time it is used.

A 20- to 30-foot, heavy, monofilament leader placed at the end of the wire line absorbs shock and lets the bait or lure achieve a lifelike, swimming action. A metal sleeve may be crimped to the end of the doubled wire and the leader tied to the resulting loop. The smaller the loop left outside the crimped sleeve, the longer this weak spot will last.

Heavy, round lead sinkers weighing as much as 48 ounces take wire line arcing down and back to lunker salmon finning at 130 to 200-plus feet. Some ball sinkers are permanently attached to the line with wire leaders or heavy monofilament with a three-way swivel. Another option permits you to fish with a sinker release that frees the heavy lead after a strike.

Using wire line gear for salmon is very effective, but many anglers do not enjoy the constant, slow cranking that's required from strike to boatside. A minor annoyance is the cost of heavy lead ball sinkers which has steadily crept up, and you lose at least one sinker for every big fish that strikes, whether landed or not, if fishing with drop-weight tactics.

In addition, rods with abrasion-resistant roller guides and tips, and the bulky reels for wire lining, are heavy, cumbersome and sometimes awkward to use. Anglers also quickly learn *not* to pinch or thumb wire line when feeding it out, or while playing a fish. Braided wire burrs or kinks in solid wire can quickly slice up a finger.

=====10=====

Artificial Lures For Inland Salmon

L ook up the word "lure" in a dictionary, and it will say, "an artificial bait; to entice; to decoy." For Great Lakes fishermen pursuing salmon, the top artificial lures imitate the water's natural forage. So, for the most part we're talking smelt and alewife look-alikes, although there are variations that do a terrific job during certain seasons.

A lure will have several characteristics that help it catch fish. Shape, color, movement, size, sound and smell are all factors in selecting the right lure for the specific fish species that you're tackling. Because we're targeting salmon, the lures used most frequently for inland fish are spoons, plugs (or hard body baits), spinners and jigs.

Spoons

Probably the most popular artificial lure for the Great Lakes, either for trolling or shoreline and pier casting, is the spoon. Found in many shapes, sizes, thicknesses and weights, spoons are made of plastic or metal, with the latter being the most popular.

Shoreline/pier casting usually involves the use of heavier spoons, allowing land-bound anglers to cast farther and cover more water. Being heavier, they sink quicker toward the bottom, where the salmon hang out—especially during the fall when their spawning instincts have drawn them close to shore.

Knowing what that spoon does underwater will help you

Outdoor writer Fred Bonner took this 25-pound, spring king salmon in Lake Ontario. He used an "Easter Egg" Yeck spoon, imitating the baitfish which had schooled in water near the lake's south shore in early May.

Artificial Lures For Inland Salmon

understand what you need to do to make it work properly. You need to know how well you're imitating the forage that these salmon are feeding on. Even in the fall when these fish are no longer feeding, the spoon still may be appealing enough for a salmon to hit it out of instinct alone. A good back-and-forth kicking action (but not spinning) may also trigger an aggressive fish to hit.

Whether you (or the fish) prefer a slow retrieve or a fast retrieve depends upon the spoon and its performance at different speeds. Not all spoons are alike, and speed tolerance will vary with each individual spoon. Get to know one or two well, perfecting their use. You'll be better off in the long run.

The same process applies for trolling. Trolling spoons are generally lighter and more elongated, but the same considerations should apply when selecting the proper bait for the fishing situation. Pick a bait you like, and stick with it. Get to know its movements, and how it reacts under various situations. Some spoons work better at slow speeds; others work well at fast or slow speeds.

In the springtime when waters are still cold, your trolling speed will be, on the average, much slower. As a result, you'll need a spoon that has good action when trolled between one and two knots. Cold water slows the fish's metabolism, so salmon won't be as aggressive as they would be in warmer water.

Many Great Lakes experts determine the size of the forage fish in the area they're fishing, and troll similar-sized bait through, or just outside large pods of those baitfish, enticing salmon that are near the baitfish. Color is important, also, but being where the action is comes first.

Scent may also play a role. For example, some charter captains like to treat their baits with everything from herring oil to the odor of smelt and alewives. They rub these baitfish on the spoon. Whether it actually works serving as an attractant or acting as a mask for negative odors, remains to be seen. Sometimes, it seems, it has made a difference.

Cinematographer Bob McGuire of Tennessee, recently shot underwater film footage, documenting fish behavior below the boat when it was trolling for salmon. Because a slower speed was needed to keep the camera stabilized underwater, McGuire's team had to be very selective as to what spoons

King salmon readily fall victim to flutter spoons (as indicated by this one that swallowed one). These spoons imitate smelt and alewife baitfish, which abound in the Great Lakes.

would work for them. The camera documented fish following a bait for two or three minutes before deciding what to do. A straight and steady troll, with a consistent side-to-side motion of the spoon attracted fish, but they didn't seem to want to hit until there was some change in the presentation process. Whether it was a fluctuation in the bait's path because of a surface swell or a change caused by the boat making a turn, an erratic motion seemed to stimulate more strikes. Something must be said for fishing on a flat body of water when it's still and when it's a bit rougher, and, trolling in straight, or "S" patterns. Varying your speed occasionally can also help create an erratic motion that may trigger strikes.

Veteran trollers will also make other changes, such as putting a slight bend in the spoon, giving it a different action. If you do that, test your lure alongside the boat before putting it down to see if the boat speed is right for the lure's action. Remember, you want it to jump and kick from side to side and *not* spin.

With spoon trolling, arguments develop about the hardware itself. Should a split ring be run at the head of the spoon, or

Stickbaits and short body baits shown here are good choices for spring action. These baits imitate baitfish that salmon are feeding upon.

should the spoon body be clipped directly into a swivel?

What about the hooks? Should you use a single or a treble hook? Personal preference makes this choice. What gives you the most confidence? Once a fish is hooked, single hooks are tough to beat especially for bigger fish. On the other hand, when a fish strikes a lure, trebles give more of an opportunity for a hook-up. Make sure that if you make a switch, the lure action can handle the change. It's also very important to make sure you keep those hooks sharp! Sharp hooks can make all the difference in the world—whether you're trolling, or casting off the piers. Pay attention to the smallest details.

Plugs

Plugs, or hard-body baits, work extremely well during

certain times of the year, especially in the spring and fall. That's not to say you can't use them to catch fish in the summer, though. Plugs have one advantage over spoons—they're three-dimensional; no matter at what angle a fish sees the bait, it still looks natural. Both size and movement of these lures imitate real baitfish.

Plugs which are made of either plastic or wood can have a small lip for shallow diving, a large lip for deep diving or no lip at all. The size of the lip and speed of retrieve-troll determines depth. They can float or sink, and carry from one to three sets of hooks, usually trebles. They can be equipped with an internal lighting system, rattles or some type of electronic signaling device. Whatever your choice, a plug may be the better way to catch fish on any particular day. With all these options available, plugs obviously are more versatile than any other type of artificial lure.

As with spoons, be sure your lure tracks properly because it is essential to the success of your outing on the water. Check not only the movement, but also that it runs in a straight line. If it tracks to the left, adjust the eyelet slightly to the right and vice versa. If it doesn't do what you want it to do, then don't use it. Small plugs may work better if a loop knot attaches them to the line. Others can be attached directly to the line with a tight knot or a snap swivel. In each instance, a slightly different action results so, again, check the action in the water. As with other lures, get to know how to run one particular bait first.

One technique becoming popular is the trolling of both a spoon and a plug off the same rod. Using a three-way swivel, you can run a diving plug off the bottom eye and a spoon off the trailing eye. It has worked well for Great Lakes anglers on various fish, including salmon. Lead lengths will vary with water clarity and depth, so experiment with different distances. Start short and gradually go longer.

The three-way swivel combination is used frequently off of planer boards, with a deep-diving plug off the bottom eye to give the presentation extra depth. It can also be used when flatlining off the back of the boat, working off outriggers or when stacking spoons over hard body baits on downriggers. It should be no surprise, then, that spoons and plugs are the two most popular baits for running off diving planes, such as Dipsy

Two-lure Fishing Rig

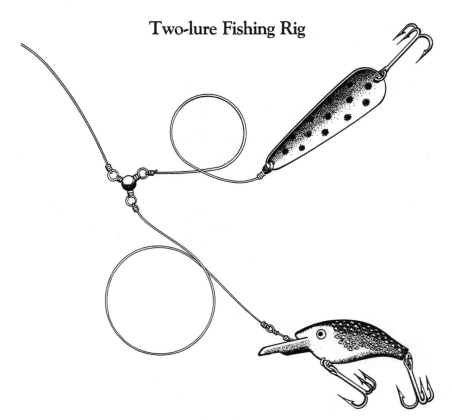

This three-way swivel rig allows the angler to fish two fish-taking lures at different depths off of one line. A combination that is quite often used is a spoon with a deep-diving plug that approximates the type of baitfish in the area.

Divers, or on lead-core line and drop weights.

Spinners

Although more often used in casting from shore, spinners have found their way into the world of the trolling fraternity. The spinner's constantly turning blade attracts attention of fish, either by sight or the sound of its sonic vibrations. The shape and size of the blade varies the vibration intensity.

Basic spinner components are a shaft, an affixed weight (or body), a hook either placed directly on the shaft or off a split ring attached to the shaft, a blade which may or may not be attached to a clevis allowing the blade to spin unrestricted around the shaft, and small beads which act as bearings to improve the blade's rotation. If a swivel is not built into the

Productive salmon spinners include (top row, left to right) No. 3 Luhr-Jensen Metric, a homemade spinner and Luhr-Jensen's Sneak. Second row, No. 4 Mepps and ½-ounce Les Davis Bolo. Bottom, blade/Cheater body rig, Tee Spoon and Salgaffo.

lure, run some type of barrel or snap swivel to help prevent line twist. It's the very nature of the spinner to turn, so this can be counteracted by some type of swivel, with a ball-bearing swivel being your best option.

Some veteran trollers use large spinners as baits or as attractors. When using downriggers, these veterans will place the spinner at a predetermined depth, then stack spoons or plugs around it to take advantage of its sonic beacon. This technique seems to work best in the spring, although it does catch fish all year.

Adding color to the spinner body or hair around the hook shank to form a brushy tail can make the lure more appealing. You can purchase a ready-made product, or you can buy the components to make your own lures. That way you can tailor the lures to meet your own specific needs, and maybe even save some money in the process.

Jigs

Although probably the least attractive lure for salmon fishermen, jigs offer the most potential for experimentation.

Artificial Lures For Inland Salmon   123

Whether it's a leadhead jig tipped with a plastic tail or a heavy, jigging spoon, either one can be very productive for taking salmon in the Great Lakes. The trick in making it work is to find the right approach, and the right area. Whether you're pier casting or jigging in deep water on a free-float, this is one approach that can be loads of fun when the fish start to cooperate. Using a depthfinder, you can pinpoint fish and place the lure down within inches of your quarry. It allows you to experiment with different sizes and colors until you can come up with the right combination.

Jigs can be made of lead or other metals. They can also have single or treble hooks, and some type of tail to enhance the presentation. You can also add pieces of whole or cut bait to further your chances of success, and make your artificial bait more real. Plastic live-bait imitations also can be used effectively on jigs.

Other Baits

Use of an attractor, such as a dodger or flasher, has added a new dimension to Great Lakes salmon trolling. Attached to the attractor is either a fly or a squid. Some flies will sport a lip creating a different type of action. They can be made from various materials, including tinsel, hair and feathers. Squid are a soft-body bait that work remarkably well in the summer and fall for salmon tricksters. Leads off downriggers may vary from 10 to 40 feet. Dragging these baits along the bottom (when bottom contours permit it) can work well for finicky fall salmon, as well as other species.

Dodger and squid-fly combinations can also work well off diving planes, drop weights or lead-core line. Short leads of 12 to 18 inches will mimic the action of the dodger. Longer leads will mean a more subtle action, which on certain days can be very effective.

Inflatable baits have also grown in popularity, but are not widely used. These baits can be used for shoreline casting or off downriggers to lure hungry-aggressive fish.

An advantage of inflated baits is that you can change the size of the bait by simply putting more air into it. It's easy to detect a strike—there's a hole in the rubber and the air is gone. The action can change by putting water or some other liquid inside the balloon-like finger. They're cheap, easy to change, and there's a wide variety of colors to choose from. The additional buoyancy will help keep the bait off the bottom. Inflatables can also assist other presentations. If you have been casting a heavy spoon from shore and you've been getting hung up a lot, try tying a small inflatable bait to the treble hook. This will help keep the hooks out of the rocks. Fewer snags means more fishing time ... and more fish. This is a new approach that NAFC members should consider.

Also, new devices make your lure presentation more appealing to the fish. A rotational lure enhancement device known as the Barney's Schooler is an advanced fishing method that allows for simultaneous, three-way lure travel.

In addition to traveling in a straight line, which may well be the least natural presentation for a lure, the Schooler also changes depth and direction. Using this type of device allows the angler to simulate the action of an actual baitfish school.

This device can work with spoons, spinners and small body baits. Use them off downriggers, Dipsy Divers, off planer boards, or for just flatlining off the back of the boat. Rotation speed is adjustable. It has proven effective for Great Lakes fishing, especially on those slow days when there doesn't seem to be any action.

=11=

Artificial Lures—
Coastal Favorites

From mountain-fed streams to the mingling of fresh- and saltwater, coastal salmon fishermen have a myriad of artificial lures from which to choose. Some of these fish enticers can be used with more than one type of tackle or technique. Of course, those who track the Atlantic salmon on the East Coast are limited to flies, but even for them, the choice is almost limitless.

West Coast—Feathers And Fur

Streamers, wet flies, bucktails and nymphs fill the bulk of compartments in a Western salmon seeker's fly box. Dry flies are rarely used, since Pacific Coast salmon normally will not rise to take surface offerings. In addition to standard flies in the above categories, yarn ties are used by a small percentage of Western salmon fly fishermen.

Most Western salmon ties are on single hooks from No. 6 to 1/0, although there are several popular British Columbia patterns that make use of tandem, two-hook ties.

Attractor patterns outnumber and outfish imitators on the West Coast. They are more readily seen by salmon in rivers often tinged by glacial melt or snow runoff. A selection of orange, pink, red, purple and iridescent blue and green patterns, most of which are tinged with stark white or fluorescent cream, often will pay greater dividends than brown, black or tan colors. Salmon strikes are provoked, in many

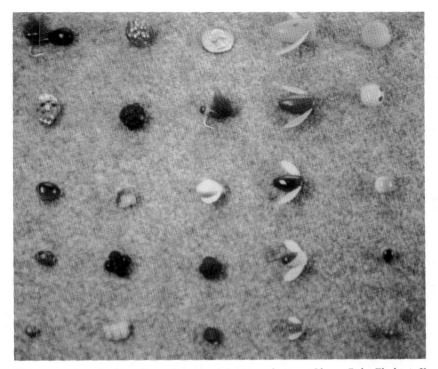

This aggregation of salmon lures shows, at left, top to bottom, Chewy Bob, Flashing & Spinning Cheater and three smaller Cheater bobbers. The second row holds three Okie Drifter bobbers, an artificial egg cluster and an imitation shrimp body. In the third or middle row are a Fenton Fly, Birdie Drifter and two Glo-Gos while the next row contains popular salmon colors and sizes of Spin-N-Glo bobbers. Last row on right has several size and color choices of Lil' Corky drift bobbers.

instances, by curiosity, aggressive habit and protection of immediate resting space or selection of spawning area.

Streamers, wet flies and nymphs also may be used with drift rigs in lieu of bobbers or bait.

Put The Metal To The Mettle

Casting spoons and spinners is an excellent way to tempt chinook, coho, pink and chum salmon into striking. Nickel, brass, copper and painted spoons are good choices for fishing large pools and deep runs where other lures may not adequately plumb the bottom. Spoons used by Westerners may be as light as ¼ ounce in weight, but most will hit the scales from ⅜ ounce to ½ ounce, with a few larger models, also.

Experience has demonstrated chinook and coho either

Artificial Lures—Coastal Favorites 127

detest or hotly desire (take your pick) nickel or brass spoons having hot orange or red finishes, either a solid back color or with natural, finish stripes slanting across their backs. The basic metal finish speckled with red, pink or bright orange spots on the back works well, too.

Coho in several rivers also are definitely suckered by a spoon having nickel finish on the belly (concave side) and white with red spots on the back. Hammered nickel and hammered brass (back pockmarked like a golf ball) are other fine choices in coho spoons. Pink salmon strike hot pink spoons.

In large waters of lakes, bays, estuaries, sounds and straits, another variety of spoons takes a large number of salmon. Made of metal or plastic, these have slight, downturned front lips and up-curled lips at the rear to give them darting, wriggling allure that has been the downfall of tens of thousands of salmon. They were designed especially for Western salmon trolling and are mostly found in marinas and tackle shops near the coast.

Casting spinners for salmon can be very productive for fish just recently arrived from the ocean and again for the same schools of salmon several weeks after they have entered freshwater. In between, there appears to be an "off-the-bite" hiatus for hardware users that lasts for two to three weeks.

Hottest spinner models are straight-shafted with single blades and weighted bodies at their center and beads or metal bearings between the blade clevis and body and between body and hook-bearing eye. These are heavy-duty spinners that range from No. 3 to No. 5 in blade size. Again, the most successful metal finishes are nickel, brass and copper. Nickel is commonly used on dark days and copper on bright days, with brass an all-purpose, anytime color.

Natural-color lead bodies will take lots of salmon. However, most spinners come with brightly painted bodies of red, orange, green, yellow or chartreuse, often enhanced with contrasting dark spots. Many successful spinners also are decorated with bright patches of reflective tape on their blades. Casting spinners are fished with upstream and cross-stream presentation, retrieving barely faster than current speed, so their blades rotate freely. A sensitive touch on your reel handle can detect the thump-thump-thump of a blade that works properly.

Spinners of a different breed are fished on plunking gear or with the drop-back method from boats. These are lightweight, gaudy, large attractors bought in plain metal finish to patterns that look as if they were caught in a rainbow's explosion. Popular with anchored boaters, especially the "hogline" salmon anglers, these spinners are used with weights that lightly hold bottom and 2-foot leaders which allow lures to seductively wave, dart and flutter in the path of spawning-bound fish.

Hoglines

When salmon schools are moving up a river, there are certain spots where experienced fishermen know good catches of salmon exist. A system of anchoring rows of boats, called "hoglines," has been developed to eliminate tangles that might otherwise be caused by boaters trolling, drifting or boondogging the spot all at once. It is quieter; fewer fish are spooked into a state of "lockjaw," and hoglines can be extremely productive.

As boats arrive, the first one to the drift or hole takes the choice spot, second boat the next best slot and so on. After the anchor has been gently eased into the water and has caught bottom, a boater attaches a large float to his anchor line which ties to the boat with a slip knot to free it.

Most anglers in a hogline will use this stationary system because they're fishing short lines, although some will use the drop-back technique. After a strike, the anchor rope and its float is cast loose from the boat, and the fisherman battles his salmon downstream, away from other lines and anchor ropes.

When the salmon is caught or lost, the boater returns to the hogline from upstream, eases into his original place, picks up his anchor float, reties the rope to his boat and resumes fishing.

Bottom-Bouncers

Salmon will nip almost any small, dark or bright, wobbling, floating, drifting or rolling object you could possibly find in a river. They will grab rocks, berries, wood chips, bits of glass, tiny pieces of metal, paper scraps, real salmon or steelhead eggs, imitation eggs and things resembling all of the above.

Why? Salmon have only one way of checking out an item to find if it is edible, or what it might be. If it looks good to eat, bounces invitingly along the bottom or smells interesting, they will take it in their mouths and roll it around between their jaws to savor its flavor and texture. So, anglers have come up with a huge variety of "drift bobbers" and food look-alikes to tempt the fish into mouthing them.

You could fill a football stadium with the brightly colored drift bobbers, wing bobbers and other egg-shaped imitators lost in Western rivers by salmon fishermen. It was discovered that these inexpensive lures held a fatal attraction for salmon. They are sold to, or hand-made by fishermen in every color of the rainbow and in myriad shapes: round, knobby, tear-drop, bullet, winged, tailed, cylindrical and a few lifelike copies of bottom-dwellers.

First made from balsa wood, and more recently from foam and other modern plastic materials, "drift bobbers" are designed to float up from the bottom from pencil lead, shot strings or bottom sinkers. The sinkers make bouncing contact with the riverbed and the bobbers (mostly used with cluster eggs or shrimp) wobble and sway downstream ahead of the weight on leaders 14 to 26 inches in length.

Some bobbers have a small, flashing blade above the lure for added attraction. Other bobbers are made from chewy plastic so a salmon will retain them in its mouth long enough for an angler to feel the fish. Still other plastic bobbers come with a sickle tail, or a hollow body for adding scent. A few lures lumped into the "bobbers" category are imitations of tiny shrimp or crayfish. Float-bobber fishing is another effective approach to fishing rivers for salmon. A top-water float can be stationary on the angler's line, pinned by a wooden needle through the center, or allowed to slide below a "stopper knot" on the main line above the float. Baits or lures wave enticingly through a drift or pool under the moving bobber. Bites are indicated by the bobber bouncing or skidding along the surface or by a loud, resounding "schwock!" as the bobber disappears into the depths.

Plugs Irritate Salmon

Plugs are excellent lure choices for angering salmon into striking. The audacious swimming attitude of these wobbling, baitfish-simulating lures can aggravate, irritate and infuriate salmon into laying some bodacious hurt on them. The Western technique used in pools and slow runs is to fish a plug from bank

130   Complete Angler's Library

Productive river plugs for salmon are, on the left from top to bottom, the U-20 Flatfish, Hot Shot and Rapala. Successful big water plugs, on the right, are Lucky Louie, J-Plug and Witch Doctor.

to bank and head of the pool to the tailout. Wary fish often will back down the current until near the lip of a tailout to avoid the sassy intruder; then, the fish seem to explode onto the plug when it reaches their position.

Flattened, banana-shaped plugs in red, orange, nickel, gold or green with black spots are good choices in rivers having light current. Pacific Coast anglers buy the models having only two treble hooks, not the plugs with wire-spreader harnesses.

Some anglers prefer to remove treble hooks and fish plugs with two single, 3/0 Siwash hooks. (The Siwash is a straight-shanked, sturdy hook with long barb and eye in line with the shank.) These hang bottom and tangle landing nets fewer times than multi-barb hooks, and are believed to have much better hooking and holding capability.

Artificial Lures—Coastal Favorites   131

Big-lipped diving plugs are also commonly used from the bank by salmon anglers. On slow rivers, these are cast and retrieved. On rivers with moderate to strong current, plugs can be fished from shore, downstream of the anglers' positions off points or from lower tips of islands.

The rigging is simplicity itself. Most Western fishermen will use an 8-foot (or longer) "steelhead strength" rod and either a levelwind or medium-size, high-quality, open-faced spinning reel with monofilament of 12 to 18 pounds breaking strength. Reel drags are set snug enough to drive hook barbs home on the fish's strike, but then allow line to be peeled from the reel spool when a salmon runs or leaps.

No swivel is used. Instead, at the main-line terminus, a positive-closure snap with rounded end is tied on and the snap's loop is fastened through an eyelet at the nose of the plug or at the back of the plug's lip where it joins the body. The rounded end of the snap allows free, swinging movement of the plug. The locked-snap mechanism is necessary because a coho will spin, somersault, repeatedly swap ends or direction, wrap itself in the monofilament and generally torture the line and lure connection. A "safety-pin" style snap often will fail.

Cast, or allowed to work downstream by influence of the current and gradual line increase, plugs are held in a likely fish lie for a minute or two, then the rodtip is moved to one side and later to the other, to cover a wide swath of water. Another 2 feet of line is run out and the process repeated.

When the drift or hole has been completely explored or the plug no longer scrabbles on bottom, the angler retrieves it very slowly, giving the fish a second chance to strike.

Fishing Plugs From Boats

A vast majority of plugging anglers prefer to fish these lures from drift boats and jet sleds. On the Pacific Coast, this tactic is called "hot shotting" (after a commercial plug of the same name that originated the practice). Guides will choose plugging over many other methods, especially when their customers are newcomers to salmon fishing and to Western rivers, because there is little a neophyte can do wrong *before* a salmon strikes. Sportfishermen also take thousands of salmon from private boats on plugs using the same technique.

Plugs are checked for proper up-down, shiver-and-shake action alongside the boat; then, monofilament line is slowly released from the reel until the plug is 28 to 45 feet from the rodtip. After the free-spool, levelwind reel is put back into direct drive, the rod butt is tucked into a holder or propped on the stern and held firmly with a foot or seat cushion wedged against the butt. Reel-drag tension is set snug enough to cause a salmon to be hooked, but still allows line to be peeled from the reel as the salmon runs and leaps.

Plugs have far better action in the water if rods are *not* held in an angler's hand. They work best when the rod is held in a fixed position. Current pull and diving characteristics of the plug provide a consistent wobbling, bottom-scratching action.

If rods are hand-held, the careless raising and lowering of a rod, or moving it when turning to talk to someone else in the boat can detract from the plug's swimming effectiveness and reduce strikes. Also, some strikes, especially those by large chinook salmon, are strong and sudden. Rods have been jerked right out of the hands of inattentive fishermen.

Stretching For Strikes

Plugs can be fished by bank-bound anglers if using what Westerners term "a poor man's drift boat." A small side planer will carry a plug into portions of the river otherwise impossible for the angler to reach.

To fish this setup, the side planer is adjusted for left-hand or right-hand operation, depending upon the current flow. Fifteen- to 20-pound-test main line is run through a swinging arm's front guide eye, and then through a rear guide eye. After a 4- to 6-millimeter bead is slid onto the line, a barrel swivel is tied to the line terminus. On the opposite eye of the barrel swivel, most anglers attach a 10- to 12-pound-test monofilament leader 3 to 4 feet long with a positive-closure snap swivel on the leader end for attaching and changing plugs.

Next, hold the side planer in hand or allow it to sit on the ground. Pull 12 to 30 feet of line by hand through the side-planer guide eyes before wrapping three to five turns of the monofilament around the guide arm. The guide arm is then locked into left or right position. The side planer is placed into the water and allowed to "swim" across the current into the desired fishing location. A skilled fisherman can work his planer or plug rig 100 feet or more into choice fish lies almost directly across the river.

A strong strike trips the locking guide arm, loosening the side planer so it will slide freely on the line, reducing line resistance during the battle.

How To "Tune" A Plug

All similar plugs, even identical models, do not run exactly the same. A plug that tracks directly behind the rodtip and moves up and down in a chugging, digging frenzy is best. Guides often sort through dozens of cloned plugs to acquire "pet" 30- to 50-fish, true-running plugs. Plugs that do not run true or that roll over often come to the surface or twist up in the line. Your speed-and-current combination may be too fast if this happens or the plugs may be too small. Either work at a speed these plugs can handle or use larger plugs.

If a plug consistently pulls to one side, it can be "tuned" to run correctly by slightly bending the eye to which the main line attaches *in the direction that you want it to go.* If your plug veers left, tweak the eye right and the lure's path will move to the right slightly. Make only very small changes.

When streams begin to give way to "big water," plugs still play a vital role in the salmon angler's arsenal. You will see lipped diving plugs change to trolling-type minnow and baitfish imitations and plugs having "dished" or concave faces. These are fished behind crescent sinkers, lead balls or on downrigger lines to attain the proper depths.

Popular finishes of these 4- to 7-inch plugs are herring scale gray, blue and green, pink, yellow fish scale and mottled pearl, or nickel, gold and red metallic. Most have white or light colored bellies and yellow-ringed black eyeballs. Hook preferences range from a single 3/0 to 5/0 at belly eye or single hooks at both belly and tail, to sturdy treble hooks in one or both positions.

Jigs And Jigging Spoons

Extremely deep holes, river spots over 30 feet, bays, sounds and straits are difficult for salmon anglers to probe with the tackle previously listed in this chapter. Jigs and jigging spoons, however, are just the ticket to put punches on your salmon record card in these waters.

Jigs, cast or forged lures, imitate the appearance and actions of injured baitfish attracting salmon strikes. Most are of lead alloy, though some are made of steel and nickel-coated brass. Two distinctive types have won wide popularity on the Pacific coast. One of these jigs has holes through its longitudinal center so it can slide on the line after being bit by salmon, preventing the fish from using the ½ ounce to 8 ounces of lure weight to throw the hook. Other jigs have eyes at each tip: one for the fishing line and one to which hooks are attached by means of a split ring.

Western salmon jigs originated in Comox, British Columbia. In appearance, these resemble a thin, elongated kite with four plane surfaces on each side and have a line hole through the lure from tip to tip. Slide a jig on your main line, add a bead or rubber bumper to protect the knot from abrasion and tie on a treble or large, single Siwash hook—now, you're ready to start jigging for salmon.

Cast from shore or dock, the jig sinks a short distance, and then the angler begins an erratic retrieve. First, the angler smoothly raises his rodtip. This is not a jerky motion, but merely a lift. Next, the rodtip is lowered to allow the jig to revolve or side-slip downward, with the angler attempting to retain contact with the weight of his descending lure. The angler takes in some line by cranking his reel's handle once. Lift, drop, crank ... repeat.

Salmon *may* smack a jig hard, but most takes are soft taps or a sudden, light feeling to the line. It is critical to strike quickly, before a salmon discovers it's not edible and spits it out.

Several other jig models slide on the line. A good representation of a plug-cut herring bait can be bent to increase its spinning, wobbling action on the drop. Some of the solid jigs with tie eyes also can be reshaped to the individual angler's preferences of S- or Z-curve contours.

Heavy spoons designed specifically for jigging or fluttering action also take a large number of Pacific coast salmon.

Squids And Hoochies

Soft, chewable, bulbous heads and tantalizing many-strip

This angler plucked this chinook with a Dodger and squid-and-tidbit trolling rig. It's a popular trolling combination throughout the country.

tails of squid and hoochies are hard for salmon to resist. These plastic imitators deceive fish extremely well and thousands are sold to Western salmon anglers. Hoochies are the Canadian counterparts of U.S. squid and are generally shorter, fatter versions, simulating the 2- to 2½-inch small baits found along the Pacific shore. Squid may be up to 4 inches long, but generally range from 2½ to 3¼ inches.

Generally used with a flasher or dodger, the squid or hoochie is baited by piercing the head's tip to thread it on the leader. A large bead or head insert is used to prevent the thin plastic from being pulled over the hook knot or eye. Bright, twinkling or reflectorized skirts often are slid on the leader below the squid or hoochie, for added attraction. Conversely, some salmon fishermen clip every other skirt strip from their

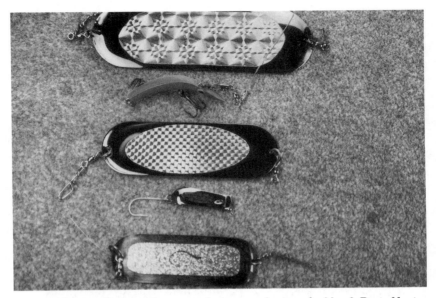

Sockeye salmon trolling rigs shown are, from top to bottom, the No. 0 Davis Herring Dodger with fire orange U-20 Flatfish, No. 00 Davis Herring Dodger with No. 4 Pt. Defiance spoon and smaller Herring Dodger with bare 1/0 red enamel Gamakatsu hook.

lure, for a more natural, lifelike appearance.

Squid and hoochies may be fished alone behind crescent sinkers, trailing after dodgers or flashers and off downrigger setups. They may be angled "as is," with whole herring baits or tiny herring triangles barbed on the rig's upper hook.

Thereby Hangs A Tail

You can get some chuckles from your salmon fishing friends when trolling for salmon by barbing a bassin' style sickle-tail or twist-tail plastic worm on your two-hook herring leader. Use only the upper hook and let the rear hook dangle. Choose a lead gray, green or motor-oil metallic flake color worm.

Watch for those snickers to turn into envy when salmon demonstrate (as they have, again and again) that they l-o-v-e those wriggly critters! Then, let your partners get off their prayerbones on the boat's wet floorboards; be a good guy and share a few worms with them.

Lures For Landlocked Salmon

Landlocked salmon anglers have a distinct advantage over

Artificial Lures—Coastal Favorites

anadromous Atlantic salmon anglers in that the fish they seek feed actively in freshwater. Where available, smelt are a staple food for landlocks; where smelt are nonexistent, the fish thrive on many other aquatic creatures including insect larvae, crayfish and leeches. This makes the angler's lure selection easy.

Minnow-imitation crankbaits are by far the most productive and most widely used lures for landlocked salmon, both early in the season when the fish are close to the surface and later in the summer when they've retreated to the cool depths of the lakes.

Second on the list of productive landlocked salmon lures is various long-shanked streamer flies. Some favorites include the Magog Smelt, Grey Ghost, Nine-Three and on far northern waters the Edson Dark Tiger and Edson Light Tiger. Though they were designed for fly fishing, trolling streamers with either fly rods or regular light trolling gear works equally well.

Landlocked salmon also respond well to a variety of silver or brass wobblers; the color and size largely depend on the body of water being fished. Trolling tends to be most effective in lakes; casting produces more fish in the rivers.

Dry Flies

Every now and then, landlocked salmon gorge themselves on emergent mayflies, caddis and stone flies. It's an event every fly fisherman should experience once in his life because there's no thrill quite like a good landlock rising to take a fly off the surface! Generally, large, bushy Wulff patterns do well during these hatches; salmon have also taken No. 6 Muddler Minnows out of the surface film.

In rivers, small spinners will take fish, but the fish react better to flies as a rule. In spring, when salmon follow schools of spawning smelt into the mouths of the rivers, minnow-imitation crankbaits and streamers are deadly. Declining daylight in late summer and early fall triggers salmon to start their spawning run and small Muddlers and a variety of small, black wet flies take landlocked salmon consistently.

Flies For Atlantic Salmon

While landlocked salmon are readily enticed to lures and flies which resemble food, sea-run Atlantic salmon are less readily tempted because, according to most authorities, these

138   Complete Angler's Library

fish cease feeding once they enter freshwater. Yet, they do rise to the angler's offerings, at times begrudgingly, sometimes eagerly.

Without understanding why a salmon rises to a fly, we have, in the course of a century and a half, developed a style of dressing which is, in many ways, unique to the world of Atlantic salmon angling. The earliest salmon flies were primarily adaptations of the handful of standard, drab trout fly dressings touted since 1496 when Dame Juliana Berners outlined her dozen, all-purpose patterns. The first major evolutionary change in the development of salmon fly dressings started in the early 19th century when Britain ruled the seas, sending its gentlemen officers across the globe.

Dazzled by the variety and color of the bird life in these distant lands, they sent exotic feathers and skins to their fishing guides and gamekeepers back home who married the materials into outrageous and flamboyant salmon-fly patterns. They were more concerned about trying to outdo each other in the intricacies and complexities of the dressings than finding a formula that would trigger a reaction from the salmon. In the process, they came up with featherwing salmon flies like the Jock Scott which, in its original dressing, requires a shopping list of about 30 different materials.

Revolution In Fly Dressings

Fortunately, salmon fly dressing underwent another major revolution during the 1930s and 1940s when a group of pioneer salmon fly tiers committed unspeakable heresy by substituting hair wings for feather and substantially reducing the size of the dressings. Since then, literally hundreds of hairwing dressings have been developed for salmon angling—most have taken salmon, a few more than others.

In terms of wet flies, some anglers insist on having a selection of Green Highlanders, Black Rats, Silver Rats, Rusty Rats, Black Doses in a few sizes. Muddler Minnows tied on salmon wire have also been good choices. Some new patterns have also been doing well—the Green Machine and the Pompier. Green Stoneflies also produce salmon consistently.

As for dry flies, salmon appear to have a special penchant for large, spun deer-hair flies called Bombers and Whiskers. They're enormous; they're tough to cast, but, if you've soaked

Examples of dry and wet flies used for salmon include (clockwise from top): dry, Salmon Irresistible; dry, Buck Bug, wet, Cosseboom; wet, Rusty Rat; wet, Black Dose; wet, Salmon Muddler Minnow; wet, Silver Rat; and, dry, Royal Wulff.

them thoroughly in silicone the night before, they'll ride proud and high across the slick surface of the pool in a way that no salmon can ignore. The original Bomber dressed with white kip-tail for the tail and wing; spun, brown deer-hair and palmered with badger hackle continues to be productive, but these days you'll find every imaginable color combination of tail, hackle and dyed deer-hair. One favorite is dressed with drab, olive-green deer-hair, white kip-tail and badger hackle. These flies resemble nothing in real-life, but they do turn on the salmon!

As a general rule, the sizes of wet flies most often used are No. 2 through No. 10; for early season spate conditions 2/0 flies are occasionally used and some anglers have gone as small as No. 16 during the dog days of August, but these are exceptions. Double hooks are used during the first half of the season when the water tends to be high and the fly sinks a bit more. Later, some anglers switch to single hooks exclusively. Low-water dressings, where the fly is tied only on the forward half of a long shanked, light-wire hook, are intended to catch salmon that rise short, but some find small wets to be just as effective. On the other hand, low-water dressings do come in handy in late August, September and October when fishing over male salmon with well-developed kypes. Tube flies, used extensively in Europe, are rarely seen here.

=======12=======
West Coast Natural Baits And Rigging

W here saltwater pokes inland along the Pacific shoreline, the very best natural bait for salmon is herring—live or frozen. While salmon also feed on shrimp, small crabs, anchovies and sandlances, herring are the main item in their diet and account for about 95 percent of baits anglers will use on big, salty waters.

River fishermen, on the other hand, use very little herring bait. Their most popular natural salmon baits are cluster eggs (derived from successful salmon and steelhead catches), roe bags, prawns, shrimp and, in some areas, nightcrawlers.

Live, Whole Baits

Anchovies are sometimes used as salmon baits in California and lower Oregon waters. They are rarely seen north of the Columbia River. Anchovies can be very effective baits when used where salmon are feeding near the surface in sounds, straits and bays. Anchovies are free-swimming baits that are most productive when fished with no, or very little, sinker weight.

Hook 5- to 7-inch anchovies by inserting your hook's barb above the upper lip of these baitfish, run the point through only the length of the barb and out again. An alternate method is to pin a hook, point upward, through the solid plate found to the rear of anchovies' gill plates. Either of these hookups allows the bait to swim freely, almost unencumbered by hook and line.

Lower the anchovy into the water upcurrent of a school of

Back-bouncing a Birdy Drifter-and-eggs combination yielded this 40-pound chinook salmon for this pair of Idaho anglers.

West Coast Natural Baits And Rigging 143

salmon and allow the strong, little swimmer to take line from your free-spooling reel. If you keep in contact with the monofilament by letting it run over or against a fingertip, you'll sense the steady, tail flips of the bait, a sudden stop, then darting flight as a salmon pursues it. When a solid weight bows your rod, crank your reel handle once to put it in direct-drive gear, then raise your rod sharply.

Anchovies are difficult to keep alive. It requires a livewell about the size of an upright, old-fashioned washing machine tub, an aerator to add oxygen to the livewell and a two-hose water exchange setup to keep the necessary saltwater fresh.

Herring

Herring are sturdy baits that can be kept alive and fresh with frequent water changes. Some salmon fishermen merely use a large plastic dishpan or rectangular tub for a baitwell. From time to time, a bucketful of water is scooped out of the bait container and replaced with more saltwater to keep it fresh.

Whole, live herring may be fished behind a crescent sinker weighing ½ ounce to 6 ounces, 5½- to 7-foot leader and single 2/0 to 4/0 hook. No additional attractor is required. The herring can be hooked across the nose just at the eye ridge or may be pinned through both lips, from bottom to top.

Your nose-hooked bait will stay alive and active much longer if you are using one of the mooching techniques. It can breathe freely and presents a lively, enticing bait. If you attempt to troll, even at low speed, however, the bait's mouth will open and it will drown.

The lip-hook method is much better for trolling, since the herring can be towed, without drowning it, at different slow speeds through the edge of a salmon school. It will appear to be a straggler or a baitfish stunned by a predator's attack and, thus, easy prey for a hungry chinook or coho salmon.

Both whole-herring hookups may be fished with two-hook leaders. For a solidly pinned bait, insert both hooks bottom to top through the same entry hole in the lips, then through the nose in front of the eye. The upper hook is barbed point-up in the hard cartilage behind a gill plate or in the upper back, and the rear hook pins to the bait's flank or is left loose. A second method is simply to run the upper hook through both lips

Hook-up Rigs For Herring

Nose Hook Rig

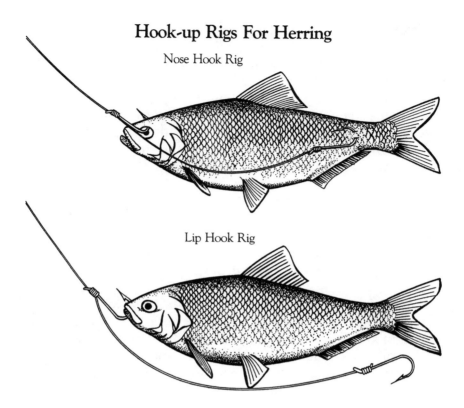

Lip Hook Rig

A standard, fixed, two-hook salmon leader offers choices of barbing whole herring through the eye ridge (top) or through the lips (bottom) and either pinning the rear hook or allowing it to trail behind.

bottom to top, then either pin the second barb in the bait's back alongside the dorsal fin or allow it to trail unattached.

Threaded Whole Herring

Anglers who choose not to tote livewells or bait tubs in their boats but still want to fish with fresh, lifelike herring, often "thread" whole herring on their leader. Fresh or frozen herring are kept on ice in a small cooler until needed, then threaded on a leader. The tool needed to do this is a long, needle-like, 1/8- to 3/16-inch diameter rod bent on one end to form a short handle and a slot or crochet-style hook at the pointed end.

The threading needle inserts through the bait's mouth, stomach and out the vent. A leader loop or free end of a leader is placed in the tip notch, and needle and leader are withdrawn. Stainless steel threaders work well, as they do not rust.

Use a 6-millimeter plastic or brass bead on the leader above the hook tie, so the hook shank won't be drawn into the bait's body cavity. Then, the hook point is too close to the herring's flank, creating a problem in hooking a striking salmon. Hooks sized 3/0 to 5/0 are the best for use with threaded herring.

Another effective rigging for inert herring is running the hook point sideways through the herring's head at eye ridge, looping your leader below the bait's jaw, going through the bony skull in back of the eyes and pinning a single hook point upward through the herring's upper back. Two-hook leaders may be similarly used by inserting the second hook through the pathway created by the first hook, barbing the upper hook into the bait's upper back or behind the gill plate and allowing the lower hook to trail.

This setup works well when you troll at slow speeds. If you're using a dodger to impart more action to the bait, try adding a bait clip or herring aid (small, curved plastic shield with hole for the leader) to the leader and over the herring's head. It helps maintain the appearance of a free-swimming baitfish following a shiny attractor.

Plug-Cut And Strip Herring Baits

Most salmon moochers and many trollers choose to fish with "plug-cut" and "fillet-strip" herring baits. Benefits include both the reflective scale flash and strong herring smell of the freshly cut baitfish's flesh.

There's an art to creating a plug-cut bait from fresh or frozen herring. With a sharp knife and a small cutting board, place the herring on its side on the board and cut just in back of the head and, in one slash, through the bait's entire body. The cut should be 45 degrees from top to bottom and 45 degrees from front to back.

Squeeze the herring slightly and its innards will pop forward, then press the knife blade down on them, stripping them cleanly from the stomach area. A perfect cut leaves no ragged fringes to the two-way bevel.

Anglers using two-hook leaders should run the lower hook point through the inside of the stomach cavity and out the

Herring Cuts For Bait

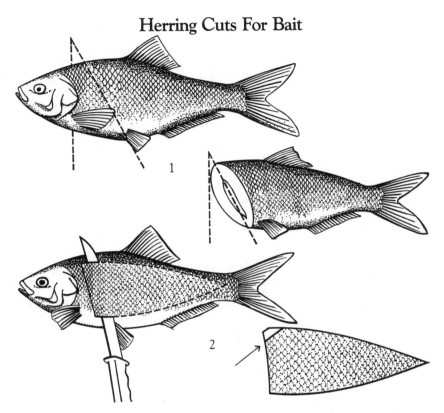

In preparing herring as bait, one quick slice (1) at 45 degrees top to bottom and angled at 45 degrees front to back produces a prime plug-cut bait. Sharp, clean edges (2) are the keys to creating a tantalizing, dancing spinner bait for salmon.

back, then follow with the second, upper hook through the same entry point. Next, pin the lower hook in one flank near the tail first and barb the upper hook on the opposite side close to the front of the bait. If a sliding two-hook rig is used, a bait can be slightly bent by drawing the hooks closer together, giving the herring a seductive roll behind a dodger. This imitates a maimed baitfish trying to right itself in the water and is highly attractive to salmon.

Cutting fillet strips (also called "spinners") is another easy-to-do method that makes an alluring salmon bait. A fillet or spinner is sliced from a herring's side (similar to filleting a walleye or saltwater rockfish). Starting with a cut behind the head from the top of the back to behind the pectoral fins, the knife blade's cutting edge is placed in the cut, rotated toward

West Coast Natural Baits And Rigging   147

the tail and run firmly along the backbone through all the rib bones back to the start of the tail. Don't trim the skin off.

Thin edges of the filleted strips should be trimmed to provide sharp front corners at top and bottom and a tiny, top corner piece is sliced off at a 60-degree angle.

The resulting strip is baited by sticking the single hook through the scale side, above the bait's lateral line, about ½ inch from the specially fashioned leading point. If you're using a two-hook leader, the lower hook would be hooked as above, with it being followed through the entry hole with the second hook. The second or upper hook is then barbed through the shoulder of the bait while the lower hook dangles free.

Nightcrawlers

If you think 40- and 50-pound salmon won't take the "barefoot boy bait" of a juicy "dew worm" or nightcrawler, it may be time to reconsider your approach. These land dwellers made meaty mouthfuls for young salmon descending their natal streams in outward migrations to the ocean, and these baits still get the salmon's attention when they come back to spawn. A good example is this story from Jim Ruppert who fishes salmon and steelhead from Idaho's Snake and Clearwater rivers across and up and down Washington to many of the rivers on the Olympic Peninsula.

"We were fishing the Elwha River (near Port Angeles on the Olympic Peninsula) in the fall of 1989 for steelhead," Jim said. "There were a lot of chinook salmon rapping our wing bobbers, cluster eggs and shrimp, so we were actually trying to find something they would *not* take and started fishing nightcrawler baits. That wasn't it! BANG! Chinook. STRIKE! Another chinook. Instead of the chinook ignoring the 'crawlers, those salmon liked 'em so much we all wound up sore-armed!"

Nightcrawlers are best fished on drift rigs with standard Western pencil sinkers pinched on the tag-end of the main line tie, or stuffed in surgical tubing pinned by a snap swivel and an 18-inch leader, terminating in one, or two, No. 2 to 1/0 hooks. The best method of hooking a crawler is to run a hook point through the head center and out the nightcrawler's reproductive ring. If you're using two hooks, pin the bait with upper hook only, and let the second hook trail beside the crawler's tail.

Complete Angler's Library

Shrimp And Prawns

Tasty and tender, shrimp and prawns make superb baits for river salmon. You can buy them from commercial bait suppliers, or collect your own. The most used shrimp baits are ghost shrimp, sand shrimp and the common mud shrimp.

A Western salmon fisherman's favorite "prawn" is a misnomer, because it is the large spot shrimp, Pandalus platyceros, which is caught in shrimp pots or traps at depths of 12 to 100 feet. Spot shrimp average 4 to 6 inches in length, although some 9-inch giants have been taken.

Anglers use only the shelled tails of these shrimp for bait. Kept on ice, these "prawns" are shelled at riverside by grasping the shrimp's head with the thumb and forefinger of one hand and the body with the other hand. A pinch and quick twist of the shell leaves a bared tail. A 1/0 to 4/0 hook is run through the rear of the tail and, then again through the inside curve of the meatier part of the upper tail.

It is a common practice to add strands of some soft, bright, tooth-tangling yarn to the prawn-tail bait when using it on drift rigs. Red, orange, pink and chartreuse are the most popular yarn colors. To better keep a prawn bait on the hook, after the tail is securely barbed, anglers open the "egg loop" or short, looped section of leader between snell and hook-eye and pull it snug around part of the tail. One special-purpose, pre-tied leader package sold on the West Coast has a short rubber band attached to its snell for holding prawn or shrimp baits.

A drift bobber above the bait makes it more appealing to salmon. Wing bobbers, especially, are extensively employed with prawns when fishermen "plunk" their gear. The fluttering, spinning movement attracts salmon, and the delicious aroma of the shelled prawn tail entices the salmon to bite.

The prawn's freshwater cousins, the common crayfish, can also tempt a salmon into inhaling a hook. Fished without shell, tough and grainy tail pieces of crayfish stay on hooks so well that sometimes one crayfish is enough for a day's limit of river salmon.

Shrimp usually are sold by the dozen in foam containers stuffed with dampened sphagnum moss to keep them alive and active. They are best kept in refrigerators set at "cool." To use one on a drift rig, hook a shrimp (unshelled) through the back of the tail and bring the hook up to be spiked again into the carapace or underside of the body organ shell.

A shrimp's claws are different sizes, much like crabs or lobsters. Even the smaller claw can deliver a nasty pinch, and the master claw is strong enough to draw blood. Some anglers pinch off the larger claw when they bait up, on the premise a salmon will take a less defense-capable bait, while others leave it on because they're looking for the biggest, meanest salmon.

Yarn strands and drift or wing bobbers also are used often with shrimp baits. Generally, hook sizes are small to match the bait's size. Hooks from 1/0 to 3/0 seem to work well, but on big rivers, hooks range up to 5/0.

"We use 30- and 35-pound line and drift rigs or plugs," a big-river guide says. "And, before heading north, I take a bunch of my rigs and plugs in and have all their split rings soldered shut. When you are battling a chinook salmon from 50 to 85 pounds, you don't want your split ring to pull open."

Cluster Eggs, Roe Bags And Single Eggs

Egg-bait salmon fishermen have a hurdle to surmount to catch salmon on single eggs, roe bags or clusters. Most recipes for preparing these baits start out with: "First, you catch a female salmon having near-ripe eggs … "

Of course, shortcuts include either buying commercially prepared clusters or wangling a starter set of egg baits from a friend and fellow angler. Egg baits from any salmon or steelhead "doe" will catch more fish, from which come more egg baits.

Each female of the salmonid species begins developing two tiny skeins of pinhead-sized eggs while still in saltwater. These skeins grow swiftly to a couple pounds of 3/8-inch-diameter eggs after the fish's return to freshwater and after the skeins nearly fill its body cavity behind the heart and lungs. Meanwhile, the salmon's stomach and digestive organs shrink to accommodate nature's scheme of fish reproduction.

A salmon's egg skeins are quickly harvested by slitting the fish from its vent to pectorals. Use only the tip of the knife so the sacs are not sliced. The skeins may then be lifted out and snipped from the stomach organs and clinging egg tract leading to the vent.

An angler "fresh out of eggs" may cut one skein into bait-

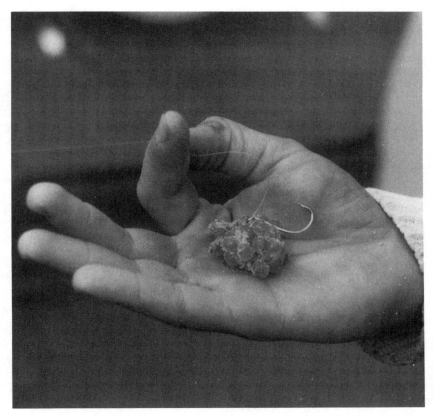

Gobs of treated egg skein work well, particularly in fall river situations. Properly treated, the skein will "leak" milk that attracts the salmon.

sized clusters right away on the bank, and drop the thumbnail-to quarter-size egg clusters into loose borax in his bait canteen. Usually, however, the skeins are gently packaged in a small, plastic bag for treatment at home.

Egg skeins have a membrane cover which is essential for the skeins becoming good cluster egg baits. Loose eggs from a ripe salmon or steelhead make better baits as single eggs or in roe bags than as clusters, because they already have separated from the membrane.

Single Eggs

Preparing loose, single eggs is a snap. Boil water in a pot or pan, add loose eggs and a few pinches of salt and simmer for two to four minutes. Ladle an egg out after two minutes and check it

Hooking Single Egg

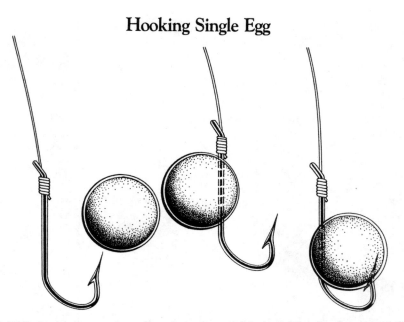

A hidden hook point near the surface of a single egg will barb a salmon that "taste tests" the tiny bait. Stick the hook into one side of the egg, and then turn the egg onto the point.

for hardness by gingerly squeezing it between thumb and first finger. If the egg is easily mashed, it is not done. If a test egg feels a bit rubbery, the eggs are ready.

A good way of storing a day's supply of individual eggs is to fill small, heavy glass bottles with screw-top lids three-quarters full of eggs; then, drop in a burning, paper match before tightly closing each bottle. A few eggs will be scorched before the flame dies out, but the burning match eliminates the oxygen in the bottle which helps preserve the eggs.

The best single eggs for salmon fishing come from chum salmon. This is because the chum salmon species has the largest eggs. Many salmon fishermen prefer coho, chinook or hen steelhead eggs, depending on their personal taste.

Single eggs are used with small hooks ranging from No. 4 to No. 1. Three or four may be strung on No. 1 hooks or fished singly on the tiny hooks. A good way to barb an egg on a No. 4 hook is to slip the point through one side of the egg and slide the egg around and up the bend and shank to the hook eye; then, turn the egg on the hook shaft and push it down again onto the hook point.

Roe Bags

Loose eggs may also be prepared in roe bags—3½ x 3½-inch squares of silk or rayon net (maline), or discarded nylon stockings and pantyhose. Six to 15 eggs are centered on a square patch. Corners and sides are drawn together snugly and the bundle top tied with monofilament or thread. Clip the rest of the bag tops off about ¼ inch above the ties. Roe bags are attached to drift rigs by spiking them once with the hook point and tucking them into the egg loop above the snell on your hook. This bait is difficult for salmon to steal because the fine mesh stays on the hook and the fine strands catch in the salmon's teeth, helping you to detect a bite better.

Cluster Eggs

When you catch a female salmon or steelhead that is nearly ripe, its eggs will still adhere to the inside surfaces of the long skeins or egg sacs, and partially to each other. This is a prime situation for one of two top Western methods of "curing" or "putting up." Handle the egg skeins carefully, so as not to loosen any more eggs, and put the eggs in a good carrier such as a plastic, zippered bag for the trip home. Store the eggs on ice in a small cooler if the trip takes more than a few hours.

Your skeins will be too moist to make good bait for at least another 24 to 36 hours. You can help the drying process by wrapping the skeins in a couple layers of paper towel, then in some newspaper, and leave them in the refrigerator at least overnight (preferably over two nights).

Next, you'll need a large, sharp pair of scissors and some containers for storing the completed egg clusters. Clean, used dairy-product containers work very well. Preparing eggs for use as cluster baits is best done when you have enough space to spread several thicknesses of newspaper on a flat surface. A small picnic table on the patio, your garage workbench, or a sturdy folding card table will work.

Depending on skein size, the first step is cutting them in half lengthwise, creating two long egg strips. If you have large skeins—and some will measure 8 or 9 inches long and 3 inches deep—cut the skeins lengthwise again through the centers. Snip each strip into pieces from nickel to 50-cent-piece size, making sure each piece or cluster has some skein membrane still

Preparing Egg Clusters

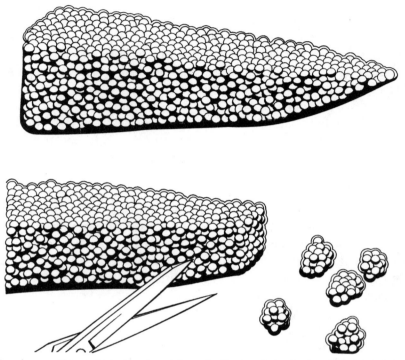

Egg clusters, if properly prepared, can be a deadly river bait. Anglers find that a juicy, aromatic egg cluster about the size of a quarter is a dynamite bait for those fall salmon.

attached, keeping the eggs together and providing a surface for the hook point.

Now, you can "cure" the cluster eggs with borax powder, sodium sulfite or a pre-mixed commercial product. Spread a quarter-inch-thick layer of powdered borax on a clean newspaper and, as you snip each cluster bait, roll it in borax several times.

After all the clusters have been cut and rolled in borax, allow them to dry for another 15 minutes on the newspaper. Then, pour a layer of borax into a bait container, followed by a layer of clusters, and another borax layer and so on, finally topping the container with more borax. Mark the date you prepared the eggs on the container lid and place them in a refrigerator for another 24 to 36 hours. Then, move them to a

Complete Angler's Library

freezer; they are relatively odorless. Take one or two containers along on each fishing trip, using the oldest cluster eggs first.

Cluster eggs are put on drift rigs by running a hook point through the cluster's skein; then, slide the eggs up the hook shank, open the egg loop of the hook snell and tighten the leader on the cluster. Generally, clusters are fished with red, orange, pink or chartreuse yarn, which is knotted to or slid through the egg loop. The colored yarn is an attractant and also helps open the bait loop. Hook sizes normally range from No. 1 to 5/0.

Sodium Sulfite And Commercial Egg "Cures"

For brightly-colored, slightly juicy eggs, use sodium sulfite or a pre-mixed commercial cure. This takes more equipment, time and care, but can enhance the eggs' strike appeal.

After cutting clusters to size, spread them out in a single layer in a flat, glass dish and sprinkle lightly with the commercial cure or the sodium sulfite mixture. To make this mix, fill an old, large salt cellar with a well-shaken combination of one part table salt, one part sugar and 1½ to 1¾ parts sodium sulfite. Turn the clusters over and dust them on the opposite side.

Store the dish of clusters in a refrigerator for 8 to 14 hours, periodically checking them and pouring off juice released from the eggs during the curing process. When the egg-juice release slows to minute seepage, the clusters can be placed in bare containers and stored in a freezer. (Do not add borax.)

=========13=========

Inland Natural Baits

Contributing most heavily to the rise of salmon in the Great Lakes are two primary forage fish species—the alewife and rainbow smelt—although each lake has its own personality relative to its forage base. No two lakes are alike in biomass, and some lakes have developed other key forage species to help take up the slack for any shortfalls in predator-prey relationships.

For Pacific salmon, the alewife seems to top the list as a preferred food. A member of the herring family, alewives are not considered to be native to the Great Lakes, although one expert believes they may have been native to Lake Ontario. Consensus points to the opening of the Erie Barge Canal in New York state as a more likely explanation for the alewives' appearance in Lake Ontario, reaching there probably in the mid-1800s.

Bob O'Gorman, of Oswego, New York, a forage research specialist with the U.S. Fish & Wildlife Service (USFWS), says another likely explanation was the stocking of American shad in Lake Ontario about the same time. Shad and alewives are very similar as juveniles. The alewife also had access to Lake Ontario through the St. Lawrence Seaway, but O'Gorman believes this possibility to be very unlikely. Another explanation is that alewives may have been present but unnoticed because of heavy predation by Atlantic salmon and lake trout. However, those prey populations were reduced by pollution and over-fishing.

Complete Angler's Library

Smelt are a popular addition to any bait presentation for Great Lakes salmon fishing. Smelt, alewives and shad make up a good portion of the baitfish on which hungry salmon feed.

Alewife introduction into the upper Great Lakes probably resulted from the opening of the Welland Canal, connecting Lakes Ontario and Erie. Early reports show the alewife in Lake Erie in 1931; Lake Huron in 1933; Lake Michigan in 1949; and, Lake Superior in 1955.

One of the problems with maintaining sufficient alewife populations is that alewife numbers can be severely affected by harsh winters. Continued, persistent cold temperatures (below 3 degrees Celsius) can stress alewife populations, resulting in a massive die-off. Quite likely, more than 50 percent of a given population can be lost during a lengthy cold period.

The alewife has a tendency to school and lives in open water for most of the year. Alewives spawn from early June into early July in bays and tributaries. When they're not spawning,

Inland Natural Baits 157

they prefer living in deep water during the day, and moving into shore at night.

As for smelt, these tasty morsels are commercially harvested in some of the Great Lakes, especially Lake Erie, with most of it taking place on the Canadian side. A secondary target for the salmon, these fish are not native to the Great Lakes either, although some think they were native to Lake Ontario.

The rainbow smelt reached the upper Great Lakes in 1912 as the result of a Michigan planting. They were first reported in Lake Huron in 1932; Lake Erie in 1935; and Lake Ontario in 1929. These fish normally spawn in the spring in tributaries when water temperatures reach 48 degrees. Smelt are a common target at night in the spring for anglers armed with dip nets. These fish make a tasty meal, or become excellent bait for casters, drifters and jiggers. They're even used for trolling. Although not the most popular part of the salmon's diet, smelt represent an important component of the Great Lakes forage base.

The USFWS, in conjunction with the various Great Lakes state natural resource agencies, conducts extensive surveys each year concerning each lake's forage base. Bottom trawls are taken during specific time periods every year to help analyze biomass, population levels and condition of fish fauna species present in the lake.

Recent survey information involving Lake Ontario reveals that alewife numbers are up overall, with a 53-percent increase of adult alewives from the previous year, while yearling numbers were up 10 times during the same period—the second highest increase since the annual assessments began in 1978. The alewife is the No. 1 forage species in the lake.

"This scenario can change quickly under a stressful, severe winter situation," said O'Gorman. "One concern is with the health of the alewives. They don't seem to be as big, quite possibly from being chased by predators. It may also be attributed to reduced productivity in the lake. All in all, though, the alewife has proven itself to be amazingly resilient to predation in Lake Ontario, and populations seem to be holding up rather well."

Smelt aren't as prolific as the alewife in Lake Ontario, but they're still an important food source for salmon. They, too,

Complete Angler's Library

Live bait (in this case an alewife) and a banana jig are a good combination for tempting salmon, as this young angler has found.

have held up well under predation, although fish over 6 inches—once commonplace—are no longer present in the lake. This may be the result of predation, with large salmonids preferring a diet of larger forage—something to think about when pursuing large salmon.

Rainbow smelt is the primary forage for salmonids in the shallowest of the Great Lakes, Lake Erie. Although alewives are present, their numbers remain depressed, probably due, in part, to the large numbers of predators—including not only salmon, but walleye, bass and muskie, as well.

No. 1 forage for walleye is the young-of-the-year gizzard shad, although they will consume both smelt and alewives when available. Smelt numbers are kept down by predation and intense commercial fishing on the Canadian side. USFWS officials in Ohio use computer models for predator and prey projections, as well as studying the effect of the commercial fishery upon this lake's populations. They've been assessing this lake's forage base on an annual basis since 1959.

Smelt is the primary forage in Lake Huron for salmon, but is not the most abundant species in the lake's forage base. The bloater—a small cisco—is the top forage within the lake's biomass, with about 50 percent of the lake's total population. Smelt are next with about a quarter of the lake's biomass, followed by sculpin (deepwater and slimy). At the bottom in the biomass totals is the alewife, at only about 10 percent. The USFWS has been conducting forage assessments on an annual basis in this lake since 1973.

Overall, smelt and alewife numbers in Lake Huron seem to be changing, but not so drastically as in some of the other Great Lakes. Alewives have declined both in overall numbers and in mean age in recent years. The mean age is now 1.4 years, down from 3.1 in the 1970s.

The same story holds true for smelt regarding age and size because of what's being experienced in Lake Ontario. Although numbers are up (as well as biomass), fish size is down because of younger age classes. However, salmon seem to actively select alewives which may account for a slight drop in their numbers.

Regarding the bloater, population numbers have rebounded for this native species. After population crashes in the 1950s and 1960s, they are now at an all-time high.

Alewife stocks in Lake Michigan are currently very low, compared with population numbers from the mid-1970s, according to the USFWS. The cause for the decline was a series of severe winters in the late 1970s, coupled with predation from salmon and trout and commercial harvesting.

In Lake Michigan, the alewife has had the most impact as a forage for salmon, especially for larger salmon. Alewife numbers are rebounding slightly, but the trend is not really significant. Smelt numbers are relatively low, but have stabilized despite pressure from predators. More smelt are found in the western and northern parts of the lake, probably as a result of prevailing westerly winds and the resulting cold water upwellings. There is also speculation that these areas may hold more food.

As with Lake Huron, the bloater has made a dramatic

recovery in the lake, probably because of the diminished numbers of alewives. When alewives were plentiful, they were a major predator of the bloater fry. Bloaters are now the most abundant species in the lake, even though juvenile bloaters are readily fed upon by salmon.

Adult bloaters could be a potential food source for salmon, but they prefer colder, deeper water, where they are unavailable to salmon and trout.

Alewives are of almost no significance in the huge body of water, known as Lake Superior. Generally, the lake's water is too cold, but a few can be found in warmer, shallower waters.

Smelt numbers are of greater consequence, with a 5-mile-wide band of water extending around the lake holding decent numbers of these fish—about 20 percent of the biomass. Although limited in numbers, they do make up a majority of the food source for predators.

According to the USFWS surveys which have been conducted since 1957, the No. 1 forage fish, based on overall population levels, is the lake herring. These fish have increased in numbers in recent years, accounting for about one-quarter of the food source for lakers and salmon.

Although some herring can be found inshore, most of these fish can be found in deep water. Herring may be a more substantial part of the salmon's diet, but because of the lake's massive size, there is little information about the salmon's summer feeding patterns when in deep water.

The use of smelt, alewives or other types of baitfish in a variety of rigs and techniques is popular on the Great Lakes. Some specific techniques are listed in the chapters on pier fishing and jigging.

Catching
Salmon

14

Taking Salmon In Rivers

Chinook are favorites of Pacific coast river salmon anglers. For size and superb fighting ability, no other species of Western salmon approaches the ability to awe anglers as does a 40-, 60- or 80-pound king. Successfully landing one of these tremendous sportfish is a quality experience that will linger forever in an avid angler's storeroom of memories. Any encounter with this Samson from the salt can either tie your gear in knots and leave you mumbling to yourself over a snapped line, or have you admiring the subdued, silvery shape of a truly magnificent catch.

Some Western salmon anglers fish for chinook several different ways and use a wide variety of tackle. Others simply stick with one method that works well. Providing the feel and flavor of Pacific coast chinook salmon fishing in rivers are a progression of tackle and tactics, starting with minimum gear for the walking angler's use and progressing up to a well-equipped river boat.

Fly-Fishing Pacific Coast Rivers

Fly fishing on rivers for chinook salmon generally is done with an 8- or 9-weight fly rod rigged with a large reel with plenty of backing. Sink-tip and weight-forward lines are common. Most anglers will cast-and-step from the head of a run to the tailout. A leader terminating in 10-pound break strength is adequate for most situations.

For Chuck Yeager, backtrolling with a No. 25 Hot Shot plug on the Wilson River in Oregon produced this 40-pound fall chinook beauty. This catch brought a big smile to the face of Yeager's guide.

Taking Salmon In Rivers

Prime fly-fishing water for chinook salmon is a long, slow pool or drift 4 to 15 feet deep. Runs having scattered large boulders on the bottom are ideal. Using polarized glasses works well because you can cast to individual salmon, rather than blind-casting to likely lies.

Casting For Chinook Salmon

Bank fishermen using casting gear to take hulking chinook salmon have to be nimble enough to skip over slippery rocks while chasing a rampaging fish up or downstream. They also need to be stubborn enough to dig in their heels when a head-shaking chinook wants to nose under a logjam or tree roots.

By the same token, tackle must be dependable, sturdy and of high quality. Generally, you will see salmon casters use wide-spool, large-capacity, starwheel-drag levelwind or hefty open-faced spinning reels loaded with about 200 yards of 18-pound test up to 30-pound monofilament mounted on 8- to 9-foot graphite or fiberglass rods. These sticks have sensitive tips that rapidly become stronger at mid-spine and have real muscle in the butt sections.

Monofilament line and leaders chosen by bank casters must have excellent knot strength and good abrasion resistance. Both will be tested to the limit by a chinook when it decides the Pacific Ocean was a kinder, gentler place and strokes downriver with your hook in its mouth!

Anglers who cast spinners and spoons often elect to fish with tackle near the minimum: medium-weight rods, large spinning reels or levelwinds and leaders breaking at about 15 pounds. Flexible lines are needed for attaining distance in casting; yet, the monofilament must have good abrasion resistance. The lures will be touching bottom, nudging rocks and logs and chugging through grass and weeds, all of which nicks and scrapes the last few feet of line above the sinkers and lures. So, be prepared.

Check Line Strength Regularly

Experienced river salmon fishermen "touch test" their line every 30 minutes or so, or after about 20 casts, to see if there are any frayed spots near the lure. Pinch the line lightly with the fingers several feet above the lure and run the fingers down the line to the positive-closure swivel, feeling for rough spots.

Any scraped or nicked area on the line is a potential snapping point when stretched by a hard-charging salmon, and should be cut off. It's best to clip at least another foot of monofilament above the weakened area, since it could be stressed. Retie with a secure knot such as the improved clinch knot or double loop jam knot.

Good casting water for lure-tossers seeking chinook is a run, slow drift or long pool 6 to 18 feet deep. The fish will lie in the seam between the strongest current and slow, "dead" water. Cast upstream, at about a 45-degree angle from the bank, probing this area from head to tailout. As the spoon or spinner enters the water, gain control of its swimming action by lifting the rodtip and starting the retrieve.

When the first vibrations of the spoon's fluttery wobble or the throbbing of a spinner blade transmits up the line to your rod hand, slow the retrieve slightly until the lure taps bottom; then, speed the pace just enough to keep it riding just barely over the rocks and gravel on the riverbed. Try to sense what your lure is doing and what kind of bottom it is tapping—mud, sand, gravel or rocks.

Frequently, chinook salmon stop a spinner or spoon just by finning over to intercept it and closing their gaping jaws on the lure. In order to drive the hook's barb home, the angler has to strike hard at least once and, if he can do so before the salmon explodes into surprised action, several times more.

Veteran salmon fishermen say the size of hooked salmon often can be "guesstimated" from the amount of time between a hard strike and a fish's first run or jump.

When The Bottom Starts Swimming ...
"When you feel a salmon surge, pull or run immediately after a strike," Chuck Schroeder, a fisherman with 45 years of salmon angling experience, says. "It probably is from 8 to 15 pounds. Bigger salmon—say from 17 to 25 pounds—sulk for a few minutes, then start swimming hard for cover or into the current. When you strike a fish that does nothing for several minutes and then, just when you begin to think you've hit a sunken log, the salmon moves its head from side to side with

pile-driver strokes, you're into a B-I-G one!"

Salmon anglers bouncing drift rigs downriver in search of chinook salmon favor casting rods and levelwind reels over spinning gear because of the baitcasting gear's greater reliability and the fact that anglers can "tail" their bait and bait/lure rigs downstream to cover more fish-holding area.

To tail or "long-line" after a cast, the reel is left in free-spool with the angler's thumb resting firmly on top of the spool to prevent monofilament from slipping out. Then, when the pencil sinker used to make bottom contact with this setup has traveled to a point directly in front of the fisherman, more line can be released by easing thumb pressure.

The monofilament will be pulled from the spool by the current. The angler gradually follows his line with his rodtip, maintaining as tight a line as possible so he can "feel" the terminal gear's bumbling, bouncing travel downstream.

Bites And When To Strike

A bite may come with a vicious, plunging dip of the rodtip. Normally, though, a chinook salmon will take drift bobbers or bobber-and-bait combinations gently, picking your offering up to taste-test and identify it. As the line quivers to a halt, only a sharp eye can tell the difference between subtle tremors of a fish bite or a snag.

Don't debate the issue. *Every* time a bait or bobber rig stops, strike. If you "turn over rocks" enough times, one of them is going to have fins! When you fish through a particular area several times, but the next drift feels a bit different, come back hard again. Sometimes, a salmon will take the hook and move toward you, creating a little slack in the line or will grab the lure and drift downstream a short distance. You should feel this slight change, and, *whenever* there's a "different" feel, strike— strike hard!

What is happening below the surface may look like this: Your leader is an average 18 inches in length. Your bait-and-bobber floats up from the bottom and is pushed along by the current, 18 inches ahead of your sinker. A salmon engulfs the lure. Until your sinker travels 18 inches past the point where the salmon took your hook, the sinker will continue bouncing bottom. That's 36 inches of sinker travel before the

Sliding Sinker Rig With Drift Bobber

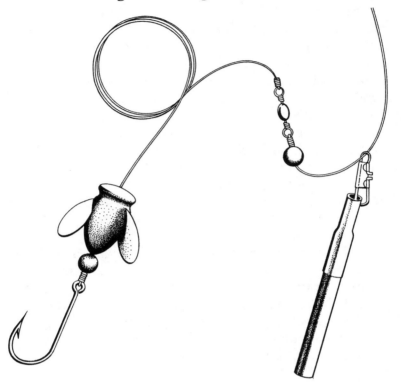

A sliding sinker rig such as the one shown here is the perfect tool to fool salmon testing your bait. The fish won't sense the sinker weight, but the angler will quickly feel the strike.

salmon's movements can be felt through the line and rod.

In that distance, the salmon could have dropped the lure or expelled it. This is why experienced salmon fishermen keep their hook points "sticky sharp," and also why they use strands of soft, teeth-tangling yarn on a large percentage of bobber and bobber-and-bait combinations. The yarn strands catch in the salmon's teeth, keeping the hook in its jaw area a little longer. This gives you more time to sense a bite and strike.

Plunking Rigs

Switching your fishing technique from casting to plunking for chinook salmon is simply done by changing terminal gear on a medium or heavy rod with a dependable reel. Clip off the snap swivel and replace it with a treble swivel.

Notice that two of the swivel eyes are in line and the third is at the base of a "T." Tie your main line to one in-line swivel eye and knot a 16- to 20-inch leader to the opposite swivel eye. From the remaining swivel eye, suspend a lighter, 24-inch leader with a pyramid or drop sinker that will hold bottom in your selected fishing area. These sinkers range from ½ ounce up to several ounces and are available at most tackle shops and marinas on the West Coast.

Good plunking spots can be located by watching chinook salmon splash and roll early in the morning or late evening. Determine where you can cast to the inside of a current favored by the fish and pitch your plunking rig slightly upstream from that spot. Let the sinker settle to the bottom, tighten up your line, slip the rod butt into a holder spiked into the bank beside you, and you're set.

Baits such as cluster eggs, roe bags or shrimp generally are fished with yarn strands, yarn and round drift bobbers or wing bobbers and *no* yarn. (The yarn can bind between the bottom of the wing bobber and leader, stopping this attractor from spinning.) It's a waiting game when an angler places his gear in the salmon's traveling lane and allows them to come to the hook. Good planning and placement lead to productive angling.

Back-Bouncing And Drop-Back Boat Techniques

Salmon anglers who find holding or traveling river stretches preferred by chinook also may hook these heavyweight bruisers from boats anchored upstream of these selected spots. The tackle used is very similar to plunking rigs except that lighter pyramid sinkers (or ball sinkers) are used.

Bait and wing-bobber combinations are common and popular for back-bouncing or drop-back fishing. They're fished over the stern of an anchored boat, with only enough line released to contact bottom and allow sinkers to settle. After fishing that area for several minutes, the angler lifts his rod and "walks" the sinker downstream another foot or two, letting a bit more line slip from under his thumb. Pausing to fish a few minutes at each extension of line, he can explore the whole river stretch for willing biters.

This technique requires constant attention from the angler,

and the rod can't be in a holder. He may also choose to keep track of delicate bites by grasping the line just in front of the reel and pulling it sideways a few inches where it is lightly held between finger and thumb. A bite pulls the line loose, and the angler follows the bite with his rodtip, allowing the salmon to get a firm grip on the bait. When there is a steady tug on the rod, it's time to strike.

Variations of the drop-back and back-bouncing technique are to fish the bait and wing bobber under a big-lipped, hookless diving plug or behind a small diver. If you're using a plug, tie a leader about 3½ feet long to the belly eye of the plug. Leaders 4 to 4½ feet long are used with divers. Again, each rig is fished close to the boat for a few minutes, then freed to back downstream another couple feet until a salmon takes it, or that section of river has been thoroughly fished.

The next tactic for boat fishermen might be plugging. Covering the water from bank to bank and head of the run to tailout should aggravate a chinook into chewing on such a face-flapping invader.

When you are positive chinook are holding where you are fishing but they aren't eating your plug, try giving them a little meat with the lure. Switch to a banana-shaped wobbling plug and add a "wrapper" of herring, smelt or anchovy to the belly of the plug. This is done by filleting a baitfish and tying a fillet, scale side up, to the plug with several wraps of thread or light monofilament line.

Some anglers remove the belly hook to get a tight, flush wrap and then screw the hook-eye back through the fillet flesh. Others slice the fillet strip lengthwise so it can be positioned around the belly hook. (If you remove the hook-eye too many times, you may find a hefty fish pulling the loosened hook out of the plug.)

This "sweetened" plug is carefully fed into the current behind or beside the anchored boat on about 18 to 30 feet of line. You will feel the plug's lip tapping bottom as it sputters and struggles in the current. As in the drop-back system, more monofilament is let out in order to search out downstream holding spots of salmon until the plug will no longer hold near the bottom.

Floating Drift Fishing And "Boondogging"

There are days when salmon choose not to reveal their lies and fishermen have to embark on "search and engage" missions. Gather your drift-rig tackle and climb aboard a drift boat or jet sled. The plan is to move downriver between launch ramps and sample the best holding spots until salmon are found. This can be done by anchoring in likely holes and casting as described earlier in this chapter, or by fishing while floating downriver.

Casting anglers generally choose to allow their boat to go downriver parallel to the bank, riding edges of the main current and fishing slack current lies on one or both sides of the boat. When willing chinook are encountered, the drift boat oarsman will drop anchor and all members of the party fish hotspots until the bites cease.

Another easy way of finding salmon is "boondogging" along the edge of main current with the boat floating sideways and fishermen trailing drift rigs behind. This technique is often practiced by fishermen using jet sleds, since they can easily zip upriver to sections producing a good bite and go through those areas again. However, drift boats are on one-way trips unless someone leans on the oars to move the boat back upstream to a good hole.

Coho Salmon

Coho salmon are a delight to tackle in West Coast rivers. They are aggressive, swift and agile, as well as prone to short biting periods separated by hours in which they will seemingly ignore all baits and lures. When they are ready to strike, though, you can't fish a fly, spoon or spinner fast enough to keep it away from coho that want to snap it up.

For two or three days after arriving in freshwater, coho retain strong feeding instincts attuned to tidal changes. A school of silvers 30 or 40 miles from saltwater and well up into its natal stream will go on biting binges that can be estimated by checking tide-table booklets. They still will bite at the times of low slack and high slack tide even though the tide has no effect on the river current where the fish swim.

Since silver salmon prefer tributary streams for spawning, rather than main channels of larger rivers, they have a tendency

NAFC Member Norman Woods took this 11-pound coho on a green Pixee spoon, baitcasting from the bank of Alaska's Kenai River.

to "stack" below mud, sand or gravel deltas at the mouths of these feeder streams. Excellent fishing can be found there when casting drift rigs, spoons, spinners or flies. "Plunkers" do very well from the bank and from sand and gravel bars immediately downstream of tributary flows. Fishermen who anchor over the deltas and place baits, jigs and lures into the first drop-off below these feeder streams often find superb angling.

Cluster-egg baits and roe bags are top rigs for catching silvers. Most anglers add an orange or fluorescent peach, round or winged drift bobber to the leader and use orange or chartreuse yarn strands with this combination.

Coho also are tricked quite easily with No. 3 and 4 nickel and brass spinners fished in slow runs and eddies. They also swat nickel and brass spoons.

Taking Salmon In Rivers

Plugging For Silvers

Western anglers like to take coho on plugs, largely because there's no indecision about whether or not a fish has taken a plug, such as with bait or bottom-bouncing lures. Coho salmon definitely pound bright, colored plugs which are danced tantalizingly in front of them in a river. Anglers often enjoy fast and furious action when fishing these darting, wobbling enticers. Best coho plugging spots are chest-deep runs, tailouts above riffles, long, slow pools and downslopes of quick drop-offs.

Big-lipped, quick-diving plugs 3 to 6 inches in length draw smashing strikes from belligerent coho which are goaded by the "in-your-face" antics of these impertinent plastic pieces. Coho can strike so hard and swiftly that your rod will be still bowing to the first impact while the silver is breaking surface 40 feet from where it hit the plug!

Choosing a metallic green or blue plug (with or without fish scale pattern), or a lure with a pearl, perch, crayfish or trout finish will generally satisfy coho salmon. Many anglers fish plugs with the maker's original pair of treble hooks. Some anglers change the trebles to 2/0 or 3/0 single-barb Siwash hooks. Drop the plug into the water behind your boat and watch it "swim," checking its action. If the plug swims true, let it out about 18 to 40 feet behind the boat; make sure your reel is in gear and drag set is correct; drop the rod's butt into a rodholder, and you are fishing.

When a determined coho strikes the plug, there is no doubt you've "been bit." Your rod will either flatten out to point at the streaking, bouncing salmon or, if the fish is parallel to the boat stern as it hits, your rod will straighten up, then begin savagely sawing up and down in 3-foot jerks.

Chum Salmon

Chum salmon are fewer in number than most of the other Pacific species and seemingly more difficult to coax to the hook. However, once barbed, they make long, slashing runs and have a great amount of stamina. Bulldog-strong, they are tough opponents to subdue. When taken from saltwater or soon after entering spawning rivers, they are still good to eat.

Touted as "hardware fish," chums will savagely attack

spoons or spinners cast above and to their lie positions. They also hit for short periods of the day when fished with lime, peach or chartreuse bobbers and matching yarn and shrimp or cluster-egg bait.

Chums favor slow river runs of 5 to 15 feet. Often, chum salmon will also be found in drifts, pools and runs below the inlets of small creeks. Water only 3 feet deep can hold a surprising number of chums, especially if there is good spawning gravel.

Pink Salmon

West coast salmon anglers find happiness when a run of "humpies" moves into rivers near them. Although one of the smallest Pacific salmon, pinks are tender eating and, if fished with tackle allowing them to display their bouncy best efforts, can be exciting opponents.

Think back to some of the bigger bluegill, bream or crappie you have taken and the excellent fights they furnished you. Now, multiply that by 15 or 20 times and you can visualize the quality battle high-sided, male humpies will give you on 4- or 6-pound-test monofilament and a 6½- to 7-foot trout rod!

Most Western streams below the Canadian border have only "odd year" runs (i.e., 1991, 1993, 1995 and so on) of humpback salmon, possibly because of some unknown river catastrophes of the past. However, British Columbia and Alaska anglers see pinks making strong returns every year. Best of all, pink salmon can be caught easily from the bank of any river they're using, because their travel routes generally are close to shorelines. Boats are useful, though, to reach spots where there is no public bank access or trees and brush prevent fishermen from finding casting room. In such cases, the boaters generally anchor in the middle of the river and cast back to the humpies' shoreline pathways.

There is a "magic hour" on good humpie streams that never fails to thrill experienced pink salmon fishermen. As dawn's colorful fingers streak the mauve sky with rose and gold and Canada geese rise honking and crying from overnighting fields, pinks will often leap, twist and splash back onto the river's surface. More awesome yet is a huge school of humpies circling a large, deep river hole.

Taking Salmon In Rivers   175

Like a ballet line, in near-perfect timing, row after row of porpoising pink salmon work upstream from the hole's tailout to its head, repeating their arcing rolls every 25 to 40 feet. Then, the school will swing across the current and porpoise downstream again. This scenario will be carried out several times, with the humpies gradually quieting as the sun comes up. This is a good time to pause to savor a cup of coffee and watch this marvelous show—because the fishing generally isn't good while parading pinks are on review. However, veteran river anglers also know that a great morning of fishing normally starts about 15 to 20 minutes after the humpies end their show.

Humpies "Think Pink"

Just like the statement attributed to automaker Henry Ford that his customers could have any car color they wanted "as long as it was black," you can tell when a good run of pink salmon has arrived in a nearby river by the sudden disappearance of pink lures from nearby tackle shops. Casting spoons, large thin-bladed trout lures, little plugs, winged drift bobbers and even pink yarn all appeal to this 3- to 10-pound salmon.

It's really not necessary to use live bait for pink salmon, but some anglers like to spike a sand shrimp on a hook, below a winged bobber; and they do extremely well with this rig.

Plunking

One of the easiest and most enjoyable ways to take pink salmon is by "plunking." An 8- to 9-foot medium-weight rod with either a levelwind reel or open-faced spinning reel and line testing about 12 pounds is standard.

Rigging begins with a three-way swivel on the main-line end; then, a 2-foot, 10-pound-test leader sporting a No. 4 or No. 6 pink and wing bobber-and-shrimp combination is tied directly in line with the monofilament. A sinker dropper (use monofilament of lighter weight than either line or leader) of 16 to 18 inches is attached to the third swivel eye, and a small pyramid bottom sinker or pencil lead sinker is added. Almost invariably, anglers use a 2mm to 4mm red or pink plastic bead between the rotating bobber's bottom end and their hook knot, to provide a bearing on which the lure can turn smoothly. A small, banana-shaped pink, orange or red plug instead of the

Rigging Up For Taking Humpies

Plunking for "humpies"—those tasty pink salmon—can produce some fine catches on a wide choice of baits or lures, as long as that bait is anchored with a heavy pyramid sinker in the pathway of upriver fish runs.

bait and bobber also might be fished on plunking gear.

The next step is casting upstream at about 40 to 60 degrees from the bank to where the main current brushes against "softer" water. Allow the sinker to settle on the bottom; then, tighten your line by reeling. Adjust the reel's drag so a fish can pull off line but the current won't. Now, you can ease the rod butt into a holder spiked into the ground and settle back with a cup of coffee to wait for the salmon to come to you.

When a humpback salmon grabs the hook, the rodtip will nod vigorously and the rod will bend severely as the fish streaks off with the bait. When salmon are nipping at the lure instead of striking, however, the rodtip might only twitch a few times and then cease moving. These light biters can be detected, but you have to be looking at the rod to see the delicate signals.

One way to ensure that a gentle nibble draws your immediate attention is to clip a tiny bell to the rod about a foot below its tip. One head shake from the fish and the bell tinkles.

Driftin' For Humpies

Another excellent fishing rig for pinks is the Westerner's standard drift setup—same rod, reel and line as for plunking, but with a single barrel swivel-and-snap combination at the line's terminus. A ¾-inch-long piece of ¼-inch-diameter surgical tubing pins to the opened snap by stabbing it through one side of the tubing. Then, a "pencil lead" sinker inserts into the bottom-end of the surgical tubing.

Other fishermen choose to thread their main line through the loop of the tubing's snap swivel, allowing it to slide freely until stopped by the barrel swivel which connects line with leader. This tie allows salmon to take a bait or lure without feeling sinker drag, but requires a fine-tuned feel for strikes.

Use just enough lead to bounce along the bottom. Tie an 18-inch leader to the lower loop of the swivel (not to the snap) and use a winged bobber, bobber-and-bait combination, small plug or a pink, thin-bladed trout lure.

This terminal gear is cast to the edge of the fast current and allowed to waddle, bounce and drift downstream while the angler feels the sinker's travel through his spinning rodtip's action and the finger grip or his thumb on a levelwind reel spool. A sudden stop in the sinker's travel, twitches or shaking of the line between water surface and rodtip, sharp nods at the rodtip or a fish's tailbeat pulsations which are felt by hand or thumb indicate a bite! A quick, solid strike will slip your hook point home.

Drift-rig fishing for humpbacked salmon also can be done from a boat anchored close inshore or in the middle of the river. The key is to fish inside the "shoulder" of fast water rubbing slower current, because that is where the pinks will lie.

Pink Spoons For Pink Salmon

More river salmon anglers will fish for pinks with spoons than other types of lures. Six ⅜-ounce to ½-ounce spoons, having solid, "hot pink" color on their backs, and a few positive-closure snap swivels, are all the pieces of tackle needed for a day of successful and enjoyable angling.

Three common shapes of spoons deliver lots of humpie action. A fat, stubby "teardrop" shape works best in slow water. Next, there's a standard shape familiar to many anglers which most effectively rides currents of medium-speed. Finally, a long, narrow, spoon shape gets down quickly through fast currents into the pink salmon's strike zone.

Lightweight, steelhead rods and medium, trout rods work well when fishing spoons for humpies. A spinning reel casts these lures more easily than a baitcasting reel, especially when 4- to 6-pound-test line is used. That's a good weight for achieving the greatest casting distance, in fairness to the size of most pink salmon. With this gear, even 3-pounders give you a tremendous but short scrap, while a maturing, humpbacked male of 8 or 9 pounds gets awesome sideways leverage from his new, "highrise" body shape.

Runs and drifts of 4- to 8-feet deep are best fished by casting a spoon upstream at 30 to 40 degrees from the bank and quickly engaging the reel to retrieve it just off the bottom. Let the spoon swing slowly across the current at the end of its downstream travel before starting to retrieve it gently, keeping your rodtip close to the water. Pinks often seize a lure when it is only a few feet from the rodtip. Generally, it's not necessary to strike hard when a humpback salmon takes a spoon that is being retrieved. Merely lift the rodtip firmly.

Deep holes in the bends or along steep banks often yield the best pink salmon angling to deep-digging spoons. Excellent catches occur by casting a spoon across the head of the hole, allowing the lure to sink and then twitching it seductively near the bottom. Sometimes, pinks will grab the spoon as it sinks, so be ready for sudden line shakes or a feeling that your lure never reached bottom. This is one time when you should use a quick, hard strike to drive the barb home.

In unusually deep spots, such as 30- or 40-foot holes below bridge pilings, try the light-tackle jigging method of fishing described in Chapter 19.

15

Fly Fishing For Atlantic Salmon

tlantic salmon are a wonderful enigma. They enter
the coastal rivers of eastern North America strong
and fresh from the oceans, pressing on up through
crystal pools with single-minded intent. Along the
way, they refuse to feed; and, yet, they rise readily to an
unlikely concoction of fur and feather, tinsel and steel.

Why salmon rise to a wet fly, swimming just under the
surface or riding on it, nobody knows, though there are as many
theories as there are fly patterns. The most believable theory is
that flies provoke a latent memory of the salmon's early life in
the river's eddies and currents when the stream's living
creatures sustained the parr's voracious appetite. Others say
salmon react to flies through instinct, clearing the stream of
creatures which might compete with and even destroy its
offspring. And, then, there are those who believe that salmon
rise to the fly during a mood swing.

All the theories are plausible because salmon react to the fly
in various ways. Sometimes, they will ignore a veteran angler's
countless expert casts only to rise seemingly deliberately from
the lie to take a beginner's inept presentation. Sometimes,
they'll refuse every offering for a period of several days; and,
then, apparently in a different mood, they'll rise randomly to
any fly that sweeps the lie.

Because Atlantic salmon do not feed in freshwater, and
because they are unpredictable, the salmon angler has the

This fly fisherman is well prepared for a great fishing experience as he takes a nice black salmon from the Miramichi River in northern New Brunswick.

Fly Fishing For Atlantic Salmon   181

greatest success odds following a series of time-tested techniques. First of all, it's essential to know where salmon lie in a river. As is the case with most salmonids, Atlantic salmon favor cool, oxygen-rich pools; although unlike trout, they do not vie for the best feeding stations. Salmon favor swift waters where ledges and boulders break the current's flow, and lie in the seams of fragmented current.

Resting And Holding Pools

Some areas are best designated as resting pools while others are holding pools; the designations speak for themselves. Salmon are most likely to rise to a fly in a resting pool because they are on the move and excited; under optimum water conditions, the fish rarely tarry more than 24 hours in a resting pool. On the other hand, they may linger days, weeks and even months in holding pools. Some of the more famous holding pools like the Million Dollar Pool, created by the influx of the Patapedia River's cool current into the Restigouche River, holds more than 500 large salmon during the summer months.

Further complicating the issue, a river normally has a mix of high-water and low-water pools. As the names suggest, high-water pools hold fish when the river is high, and the others hold fish when the river is low. The current's flow, the amount of dissolved oxygen and the availability of lies are more important than water depth in the salmon's pool selection. This explains why some of the best-looking (to the angler) pools are barren for most of the season, while others, unsatisfactory to the angler's eyes, hold fish all summer.

Knowing the holding pools, the resting pools and the high-water and low-water pools of a river is the first step to finding salmon. Knowing where the fish lie is the next step. There are no rigid rules determining the best lies, but Atlantic salmon tend to gravitate to the pool's head and tail where the current is better, even though there may be excellent lies along the entire length. Polarized sunglasses are a tremendous help for spotting salmon in these pools.

Disclosing Their Lies

Salmon frequently show themselves by rolling (porpoising), flashing and jumping. All three help the angler locate fish in a

These two Atlantic salmon, shown in the center of the picture, are resting in a shallow pool. The trick here will be to get them to rise to a fly. The angler should work the pool systematically so as not to spook these fish.

pool, though the latter is the least desirable display since a jumping salmon is least likely to take a fly. The head-to-tail rise of a rolling fish, on the other hand, is a good sign since it indicates that the salmon is anxious or alert and might be enticed to rise to a fly. At one time, local anglers believed that salmon flashed in order to scrape sea lice from their sides, but biologists now suggest that the Atlantics' flashing is a mock-spawning ritual. The flash of the broad flanks of bright fish is easier to see than that of a stale salmon whose sides have tarnished from weeks and even months in freshwater.

Whether the salmon show themselves or not, there is a system to working the pool. The wet-fly fisherman starts at the head of the pool, well up in the rapids and casts the fly at a 45-degree angle to the current. On the first cast, the fly line should not extend more than about 10 feet beyond the tip of the rod since the salmon might be virtually lying at your feet. Let the fly swing through the current until it is directly downstream, then pick it up and cast again at 45 degrees to the current, extending your line by about a foot.

Repeat the process until you've reached either the outer edge of the current or a cast length that you can comfortably control; it's more important to lay out a clean, straight line than a lot of line. Once you've reached your maximum cast, move down a step (2 to 3 feet) and cast again, letting the line swing around until it is directly downstream; then, take another step downstream and cast again.

Sweeping The Pool

At no point should you change the fly line's length. The purpose is to sweep the entire pool thoroughly. And, as the fly nears the end of the swing, start to strip in some line so the fly does not hang motionless in the current at any point. Frequently, salmon follow the fly around and, if the fly speed changes, the fish turns away.

There are no iron-clad rules governing how quickly you should work the pool. Some anglers pick it clean, covering every square inch with their fly by moving downstream half a foot at a time; others cover it quickly, 4 or 5 feet at a time, thinking a taking salmon will come for the fly from quite some distance. It seems to depend largely on conditions. If the salmon are fresh from the sea and water conditions are right, a pool can be worked quickly. On the other hand, stale salmon are less brash and need extra coaxing.

Fishing By Canoe

On big rivers like the Quebec's Matapedia, Cascapedia and Moisie, as well as New Brunswick's Restigouche, anglers fish from canoes. Essentially, the method of covering the pool is the same except that the canoe moves down through the current and you fish from given stations called drops. In this situation, the guide starts by anchoring the canoe at the head of a pool. While he sits low in the craft's stern, to prevent being a target for dropped back casts, the angler sits or stands at the bow and starts casting, usually to both sides of the canoe. The first sweep cannot be too short; many guides have admonished their clients for starting too far out and many anglers have been startled when large salmon rise to the fly that is barely 3 feet off the canoe's bow.

In fishing from a canoe, the angler lays one cast at 45 degrees to the current off one side of the canoe, and then does the same on the other side. Before the next cast, the line is extended a foot and the pattern repeats until the angler is at the full extent of a comfortable cast. At that point, the guide either opts to change flies or lift anchor and drift down to the next drop; then, the angler starts again with a short line and extends it a foot at a time to sweep the water around the canoe.

A popular variation on the standard wet-fly technique is to use a Portland Hitch to skate the fly across the surface. Essentially, the Portland Hitch consists of one or two (most prefer two) half-hitches thrown over the fly's head, and tightened so that the leader extends from underneath the fly. When a fly with a Portland Hitch is cast over the pool, it rides up on the surface, creating a wake. On most Newfoundland and Labrador rivers, the hitch is used almost exclusively, and worth a try on virtually every salmon stream.

In all wet-fly fishing, the fly speed is probably the most critical single aspect in salmon fishing. If the fly travels too slow, the fish will show little or no interest in it; if the fly moves too fast, the fish may rise to it but miss, or the fish may only rise part way and then change its mind. In a normal, steady current, a 45-degree cast sweeps the fly at just the right speed; when the flow is slower, the fly speed can be increased by laying the cast further upstream, that is, at closer to 90 degrees to the current. By the same token if the fly moves too fast, the speed can be reduced by casting a sharper angle to the current. In cases where the current is not strong enough to provide the proper fly speed, the angler can help by stripping in line.

Demands Full Concentration

Atlantic salmon angling is a game of concentration. The angler's attention must be riveted to the fly and the water around it at all times. Frequently, a salmon may move to the fly without actually taking it the first time around, but if the angler does not see that and continues moving down through the pool, the fish eventually spooks and loses interest. Sometimes, the fish reacts to the fly with a head-to-tail roll; other times only the snout appears behind the fly but the rise might be even more subtle. Often, it's no more than a suspect bulge of water behind the fly or a glint below the surface—clues which the beginner can easily miss. It takes several years of experience to recognize the subtle rises of salmon. Again, a pair of polarized sunglasses can be an invaluable help.

Several theories exist about what the angler should do when a salmon rises to the fly without actually taking it. One theory is that you should rest the fish for as long as 15 minutes; another says you should change to a bigger or smaller fly, or try a different pattern altogether. However, an angler would do just as well stripping in the line, checking the leader for wind knots and making sure the hook's barb has not been dinged off on a dropped back cast, and then putting the same fly right back to the fish, about a foot or two short. If the salmon has shown interest in the fly once already, chances are it will do so again. If the fish rises to the fly again without taking it, try slightly changing the cast's angle, changing the line speed. If that doesn't work, go to a smaller fly of the same pattern. If the salmon still does not take, try changing fly patterns altogether.

Dark Flies, Bright Flies

Some basic rules guide selecting patterns for wet-fly Atlantic salmon fishing. First of all, light-colored flies work best on bright days and dark flies in low-light conditions. Some favorites for fishing in clear water under blue skies are the Green Highlander and Silver Rat. On overcast days, the Rusty Rat seems to be extremely effective, and, on dark days, the Black Dose, Black Rat and Black Bear Green Butt work well.

Another rule of thumb for selecting wet flies is large sizes for high water and small sizes for low. Early in the season when the rivers are high, you might use 2/0 flies, but at the end of June the water levels usually start to drop and it's time to switch to No. 4's. In mid-July, No. 6 flies and smaller are the best bet. There are a couple of exceptions, however. First of all, in the fast-water runs at the head of a pool, use flies a size or two larger than you would in the steady flow of the rest of the pool. Secondly, an oversized fly will often attract attention when the

This Atlantic was taken from a stream with a Silver Blue wet fly. In fishing wet flies, speed is the critical factor. Also, the angler may find the salmon's rise to be subtle.

recommended sizes do not. In late season, when the salmon become territorial, a large streamer fly often triggers a take from a hook-jawed male.

Dry-fly fishing is another realm altogether, and some anglers say it's the ultimate experience in salmon fishing. Watching a large fish turn from its lie to deliberately rise to the fly is so unnerving that the offering is frequently yanked away before the salmon can take it. Slick water tends to be better for dry-fly fishing than heavily rippled water, because the fly is more noticeable in slick water as it floats over the fish.

Fishing The Dry

While a wet-fly fisherman usually starts working a pool at its head, a dry-fly fisherman will start at the pool's tail, working up toward the head. This is because a dry fly seems to be more effective when it surprises the salmon from behind; another reason is that, by fishing upstream, the fly can float more freely. Good fish have been taken when casting upstream into the current. However, this requires a great deal of effort stripping in the developing slack. So, the best technique is to fish cross current. Graphically, the angler stands facing the river at a 90-degree angle and casts the fly slightly upstream, close at first, and then increases the length of the line by about 2 feet on every consecutive cast until either the maximum controllable casting distance is achieved or all the water has been covered. At that point, the angler retrieves all the line and moves 3 feet upstream. He then starts over with a series of gradually longer casts.

The trick is covering all the water systematically from the pool's tail to the head, carefully probing the likely lies. A clean float is important most of the time, although occasionally a dry fly skittered across the surface will infuriate an otherwise inert salmon. One way to get a long, natural float is with a technique called the spaghetti cast. The angler casts the dry fly normally across the pool, but just before the fly touches the surface, the angler gives a slight backward pull which causes a series of undulations in the line when it lands. A looped spaghetti cast, achieved by pulling back and slightly upstream on the line, creates these same S-curves, but, in addition, the fly lands farther downstream, making a more desirable presentation to the salmon.

The greatest difficulty in dry-fly fishing is knowing when to strike the fish. Essentially, in most Atlantic salmon fishing, the angler does not set the hook; the fish does. Calling it "striking the fish" is misleading; it would be more appropriate to call it "raising the rod to the fish." In wet-fly fishing, the angler raises the rod from a horizontal position to the vertical as soon as the line tightens. It's a steady, deliberate action rather than the hard, sudden strike common to other forms of fishing. The same goes for dry-fly fishing, but novices and even excitable veterans tend to raise the rod too soon, pulling the fly away from the fish. Even though you can see the salmon take the fly, wait for the fish to turn, and the line to tighten before reacting. At that stage, the fly lodges in the corner of the mouth—right where you want it.

This angler works a pool for Atlantics on Quebec's Patapedia River. It's important to determine the fish's position so that the fly can be presented effectively to it.

When A Salmon Rises

As is the case in wet-fly fishing, a salmon showing interest by rising even a couple of inches to the dry fly is a likely taker and should be worked carefully. Once you raise a fish which does not actually touch the fly, give it a couple of minutes to return to its lie. Take advantage of the wait by checking the hook's barb, the leader for wind knots and letting the fly dry. If you can't actually see the salmon which rose to the fly, try to establish its location in the pool, bearing in mind that it probably drifted backward for several feet on its way to the surface. Depending on the force of the current and the depth of the lie, the lie might actually be about 10 feet upstream from where the fish rolled.

The orthodox procedure for working a taker with a dry fly is to annoy the salmon by dropping the fly momentarily all around it. Cast the fly above and beyond the fish, letting the fly drift a foot or two before gently picking it up. The next cast should be placed upstream of the fish, but to the near side of the salmon; again, let it drift briefly before picking it up. The third cast should go directly in front of the salmon. If the fish still doesn't move, repeat the sequence over and over until it does. A steady, well-timed rhythm is important to this technique so that the fish starts to anticipate the reappearance of the fly. Some fish react almost instantly to the technique while others can be bombarded over and over again for as long as an hour before they rise. Eventually, all salmon either come for the fly or leave the pool altogether because of the constant barrage.

A less orthodox and equally effective technique is casting the fly to a spot 10 to 12 feet directly upstream of the lie, letting it float drag-free over the salmon's nose. The corridor in which the fish will take the fly is extremely narrow; but, when you get it right, the fish will usually rise. When all else fails, try skittering the fly over the salmon's nose. Many enraged salmon have chased a skittered fly right across the pool like a dog chasing a cat.

With exceptions, the general rule in selecting dry flies is the bigger the better. Spun deer-hair Bombers as much as 4 inches long are incredibly effective for Atlantics. The original Bomber pattern calls for a tail of brown, deer-hair, a body of spun, natural deer-hair clipped cigar-shaped and stiff, brown, dry-fly hackle wound forward from tail to head; the wing consists of more deer-hair slanted *forward* at a 45-degree angle.

Since the emergence of this pattern during the mid-1960s, it has undergone many modifications, with the most prominent being the substitution of white kip-tail for the deer-hair in the tail and wing. Other modifications call for bodies spun from white deer-hair, as well as a wide range of colors. A favorite Bomber dressing calls for white kip for the tail and wing, deer body hair dyed olive-brown and badger hackle, with the wing splayed, Wulff style.

The secret to a good Bomber is using the very best dry-fly hackle that money can buy and treating it thoroughly before casting over a pool. To be effective, a Bomber must ride high and proud on the surface. Before the start of the season, soak

This good-sized Atlantic fell victim to a Bomber dry fly. The Bomber must be properly treated so it rides high and proudly on the water. Its effectiveness makes it the most popular dry fly on salmon streams. Often, the secret is to make the salmon angry enough to attack your dry-fly offering.

your Bombers in liquid dry fly-flotant—you can make your own using carbon tetrachloride, silicone and paraffin in equal portions—overnight, and then hang them up to dry for at least 24 hours in a well-ventilated area. Preparing the flies in advance ensures that they all ride well and won't need an application at streamside.

Other Patterns

While Bombers are the most popular dry flies on salmon streams, a few other patterns are worth noting. White and Black Wulffs, as well as some bright green Wulffs, take their fair share of salmon every year, especially considering the amount of usage they get compared with Bombers. Other good dry-fly patterns include the Irresistible and Rat-faced MacDougall.

Whether you hook a 4-pound grilse or a 35-pound salmon—on wet or dry fly—you'll experience a fight that few other fish can give, be it freshwater or salt. Generally, the first thing a salmon will do when it realizes it is hooked is take a long run that probably takes you well into the back-line and usually culminates in a spectacular jump (the first of many such jumps during the course of a fight). Traditionally, when a salmon jumps, the angler pays it homage by bowing the rod; that is, immediately dropping the rodtip almost to water-level and even extending the arm holding the rod to provide additional slack in the line. This prevents the fish from falling back on a taut leader and, in so doing, either breaking the leader or pulling the hook loose.

Another thought suggests that bowing to the fish is unnecessary because a flexible rod should absorb any shock created when the salmon falls back on the line. Giving the fish slack is actually counterproductive since it could allow the hook to slip. However, many veteran salmon fishermen lean toward the bowing theory. Besides, it's an act of respect that an angler owes to such a noble fish—the Atlantic salmon.

Some Jump, Others Sulk

Not all salmon jump; some, in fact, refuse to even roll on the surface until the very end of the fight. As a general rule, the bigger the salmon the less likely it will jump. That's not a hard-and-fast rule, though. Sometimes, a 16-pounder will never show and there are some hooked 30-pounders that spent more time in the air than in the water. Salmon in the 16- to 18-pound class are perhaps the best fighting fish; only grilse fight harder, but tend to be brash rather than deliberate like a bigger fish.

A lot of salmon anglers maintain that the fight should last a minute for every pound the fish weighs. But, the length of the fight depends largely on the fish's temperament and the angler's experience. A good salmon fisherman can subdue a strong fish in a matter of minutes by depriving it of even a moment's rest, whereas a beginner is often unaware of the strategies a salmon uses to conserve and replenish its energies. The length of the battle should depend on whether the fish is released.

As a result of the serious decline in our Atlantic stocks

through the 1970s, North American salmon anglers have opted to release multi-sea-winter fish—that is, all salmon with a nose to fork length of more than 25 inches—because these are considered to be the most valuable spawners. (Quebec is one of the few exceptions in not having this regulation.) Since the salmon's survival compromises severely when the fish is fought to exhaustion, anglers have a responsibility to bring the fish in as quickly as possible and to release it with a minimum of handling. Ideally, the best way to release a salmon is to simply snip the leader at the knot and let the fish swim off with the fly.

Daily And Season Limits

Another conservation measure first implemented in 1984 limits the number of salmon an angler can take during the course of a season. From an unlimited season limit, the new Atlantic salmon angling regulations suddenly imposed a 10-fish quota (seven in southern Quebec). To ensure that this limit is respected, anglers receive the appropriate number of plastic tags with their permits. A tag must be affixed to the salmon the instant it is killed. Once the angler has used up the allotment of tags, his or her season is over. The daily limit varies from one fish a day per angler to as many as four a day, depending on the area fished.

The quotas, in part, serve to reduce the number of Atlantic salmon taken by sportfishermen in any one season. At the same time, an increasing number of anglers opt to lengthen their season by releasing the majority of the Atlantic salmon they hook to avoid using up the limited number of tags. Thanks to their efforts and the ongoing vigilance of Atlantic salmon conservation organizations, North America's Atlantic salmon stocks are in surprisingly good shape and their entry into the 21st century is assured. Future generations of anglers will thrill to the run of an Atlantic salmon, still dime-bright and strong from the sea.

=====16=====

Trolling For Salmon

T rolling for salmon has received the most notoriety in the Great Lakes Basin. This chapter will provide information on some basic seasonal patterns that can be used for any of the Great Lakes where salmon are present. This will apply primarily to chinook and coho, as they are the major species found in the Lakes.

Spring

The popularity of early-season salmon fishing has risen dramatically throughout the fishing fraternity in recent years. And, more often than not, rusty anglers aren't ready for the onslaught administered by these feisty fish—primarily from the chinook and coho salmon.

The reasons are many: spring salmon that fight like a young Mike Tyson ... young, aggressive and "hungry" for a good fight; the fact that these fish are easily accessible, close enough to shore that even the average fisherman can capitalize; and, if you're after meat for the freezer, there's no better table fare than a mid-sized spring king or coho—these are the reasons why spring salmon fishing is growing in leaps and bounds.

Some sort of underwater structure is the key to finding fish, whether it be bottom, thermal or current structure. It can be any one situation, or a combination thereof, that attracts salmonids to a particular area. In the spring, temperature is probably the key ingredient for successful fishing recipes. Look

For exciting, early-season salmon fishing when the fish are in the warmer shallows, a small boat works fine. You'll notice that this angler doesn't worry about downriggers and holds his own rods.

for warmer water in the way of a sharp thermal temperature break, and you'll find fish. Then, you've got to catch them!

Three methods usually work early in the year (of which there are many variations): use of planer boards, use of down-riggers run shallow and flatlining techniques. All three will produce fish, allowing personal preference and fish selectiveness to dictate which method will work at any particular time.

Fish, like people, tend to be in different moods during different conditions or time frames (or so it seems). Sometimes salmon will act bold or arrogant, willingly taking offerings from fishermen 5 to 10 feet off the cannonball of a downrigger; however, in the spring, salmonids tend to be more wary of cable and engine noise because of the shallow surroundings. Hence, the success of surface side planers and flatlining setups.

It's these warming water trends that attract the baitfish so essential to the growth of these popular fish. Smelt and alewives make their annual migration up many of these same tributary streams releasing warmer waters. And, where there's forage, there are bigger fish nearby to feast when the time's right.

As far as the Great Lakes go as a whole, the southern portions of the lake tend to be the areas that will warm first, therefore attracting the forage fish ... and the salmon and trout won't be far behind.

Generally speaking, boat fishermen capitalize with both spoons and stickbaits that imitate these same forage fish. From shore, spawn sacks are popular, as are heavy spoons and body baits. But, the key, again, is to find out what will work.

Color selection is sometimes just as important as lure selection. Sometimes, even more so. Chartreuse and fluorescent orange are two colors that are usually "hot" in the spring. But, an Easter-egg color might do better early in the morning, or green might work best for high-pressure, sunny days.

Color patterns on the lures themselves might be the determining factor on any given day as to whether you will catch your limit. There are four different types of taping patterns that can be used: polka dot, straight up-and-down stripe, diagonal slash and tri-color. A ladder-back might be considered a variation of one of these four types, and there are very many off-shoots of these. Whatever it takes to catch fish, that's what we recommend to use. Overlays work well on certain days, too.

Keep your groups or sets of lures together, using similar colors and types of spoons. Know what you're doing with each lure, so that when you do catch a fish, you'll know what you did *right*. When you find out what that is, give it to the fish. When they're on a feed, take advantage of it. Know what direction you were trolling, what speed you were going, as well as what and where your lure was. If you have trouble remembering, write it down. It could make a difference not only for the particular day you're out, but for future outings as well.

Knowing what to do in a variety of given situations for early-season salmon fishing doesn't always come easy. Books can be written on the many "tricks of the trade" that are used on the water, primarily from charter fishing captains that make successful fishing a must if they want to make a living at it. Although each of the Great Lakes has the same basic fishing requirements, different patterns do develop that might work for one, but not another.

Summer

The place was Lake Ontario. The port, Wilson, New York. We were trolling north in search of nomadic salmon and trout in preparation for the annual Lake Ontario Pro-Am Salmon Team Tournament. Our boat was the *Bullfrog* captained by Jeremiah Heffernan, and our method of fishing was referred to as "high and wide" by the skipper ...

"Release!"

The announcement sent everyone scrambling to their positions. There was no question what the crew had hooked, and Michael Duffy was the closest to the screaming reel. He quickly reached over and forced the rod butt from the holder, not needing to take any slack out of the line—this king was carrying the mail. "Too bad we couldn't have caught this fish tomorrow," wished Duffy, referring to the start of the Pro-Am. "Let's hope the fish stays put." Twenty-five minutes later, the crew boated a nice 25-pound chinook salmon taken on a small spoon. Unfortunately, the fish didn't stay put.

Trying to locate a pocket of fish that have taken up temporary residence during this period is a next-to-impossible task. Fish are generally on the move as they adapt to seasonal transitions, no matter where you're fishing in the Great Lakes Basin. In order to be a successful angler, you, too, must also change with the seasons—keying in on various aspects of your trolling techniques to locate, and satisfy the needs of the fish you pursue.

Experienced anglers are familiar with the importance of water temperatures relative to fishing success. Pinpointing the thermal bar in the spring, and keying your activity around it, should help you produce your fair share of releases. Fish are hungry and much more competitive as far as food supplies go. As the waters warm, however, the colder, dense water pushes offshore until it reaches a point where the lake actually makes an acrobatic flip from top to bottom. At the bottom is the heaviest water (checking in at 39 degrees) as the lake begins its stratification process. The thermal bar vanishes; the thermocline appears. In the meantime, fish scatter.

New York's Sea Grant has researched this phenomena, and the earliest date a thermocline has set-in on Lake Ontario was May 1983. The latest date was July 1982. On the average, though, it's been around the second or third week of June that the lake sets up its thermal horizontal layers. Our concerns are not with the vertical thermal bar; or, when the lake's stratification has become established. We're looking at the "transition." The time from thermal bar to thermocline when fishing has a tendency of becoming extremely tough, especially for those who have little or no experience during this changeover period. It's time to turn to the experts. These same types of transitional tactics hold true for all the Great Lakes.

There are several keys to transition fishing, and how well you're able to adapt will be reflected in your overall success on the water. All of these keys relate directly to any other successful trolling patterns or techniques you may have experienced on the Great Lakes—but each aspect must be fine-tuned to meet the ever-changing needs of the fish ... as they relate to weather, temperature and wind. Your ingredients to a satisfying Great Lakes trolling recipe should be: bait presentation, proper speed, versatility, proper bait selection and, of course, location.

During the "transition," no single set technique or pattern will work for you day-in and day-out. Tactical changes must be made on a daily basis quite often, sometimes sooner. More than one pattern can work, too. While Heffernan is fishing "high and wide" off his planer boards in front of Wilson using shallow-running, Deep Six diving planes over deep water, charter captain Bob Cinelli of Lockport may be running his downriggers near bottom structure, trolling small spoons to imitate baitfish.

"Plan on things changing," says Cinelli, a Lake Ontario charter service captain out of Olcott. "This is the time of year, probably more than any other, that fish are on the move. Presentation is important, along with boat speed. In fact, speed is critical during the transition. You're fishing a program to intercept fish on the move, so you must be very particular with

Can't find exactly the right stickbait for those finicky salmon? This captain keeps a large selection within easy reach so you can keep trying different baits until you find the right one.

all your fishing components."

Cinelli should know. He and Heffernan have consistently guided their teams to top-10 finishes in Great Lakes competitions—a real test for transition specialists.

Another veteran on the water is captain Greg Gehrig of Oswego. Although it's the Eastern Basin of Lake Ontario, the same transitional changes affect him and his fishing tactics. He targets salmon and brown trout and uses his scanning sonar to identify warm water and baitfish pockets. There are no rules as far as depth and direction, but he moves at a decent pace (2.5 to 3 mph) with black-based spoons like Southport Slammers off his 'riggers 20 feet down and 20 feet back. The 20/20 approach, combined with the speed, allows him to cover as much water as possible.

"I'm looking for warm water pockets or current lines on a day-to-day basis," says Gehrig. "Nothing's guaranteed, but the 20 down/20 back presentation seems to work well for me. My speed is critical. Since the fish are cruisin', so am I."

Although all three of these captains prefer spoons, stickbaits can also work under the right conditions. Run your baits at their optimum speed ranges, experimenting to determine what baits and speeds will be working for you that particular day. Once you've found the secret, stick with it. Also, keep track of your successes (and failures) in a fishing diary. It may help you out the next time around ... or the following year.

Location

Your fishing selection area should contain the presence of bait for these foraging fish. "If there's calm water," said Heffernan, "you might actually see baitfish jumping on the surface. Once I've located bait during the transition, I'll work the edges with a lot of junk ... until I find what the salmon want. Then, I try to match spoon size with the bait ... a variety of small and regular sized spoons such as C-5 NK's, Salmon Seekers or small Andy Reekers."

Cinelli agrees. "Sooner or later, the big fish have to eat," he said. "Either fish the edges of bait pods, or intercept the fish before they get there. By identifying bait locations, you should be able to rule out dead water."

A good example of the transition fishing inconsistencies is the Niagara Bar off the mouth of the Niagara River. During past fishing seasons, mid-June coho salmon action had been next to phenomenal. In recent years, no cohos arrived on the scene at that particular location. Instead, good coho schools were found deep in front of Olcott during the mid-June doldrums. One thing that was consistent with the time period was the fish's passion for red. It didn't matter if it was a red dodger and fly combination, or a red spoon—these fish attacked with the fury of an angered bull in the ring.

Transition-type fishing isn't restricted to just salmon and trout either, and that's one reason why Heffernan feels he has an advantage. In fact, he likes fishing the "transition."

"I've done a lot of walleye fishing on Lake Erie," said Heffernan. "Many of the same techniques and patterns that I've used there have helped me with the salmon ... and vice versa." Since Heffernan consistently finishes in "the money" for major angling tournaments and derbies on the Great Lakes, who would argue with his approach to fishing the "transition?"

There are no set rules in transition fishing. Your imagination is the limit for what will work on any particular day. Pay attention to details, and keep track of positive and negative aspects as you trial-and-error your way through a tough period. Once you better understand what's happening, the "transition" may actually become a blessing in disguise.

Fall

Autumn—the end of summer. Leaves will slowly start to change into their colorful fall attire, as daylight gets shorter with each passing day. It's a time that also signifies the return of the mighty king salmon into the natal waters in which they were stocked.

For the salmon, it's one of the final stages of their life cycle. These Pacific salmon, of which both chinook and coho are stocked, live in Lake Ontario for roughly four and three years respectively. They're approaching the end of their desires to feed, and when it comes time to spawn, their stomachs will actually shrink in size.

It is during this time period that these mature fish will become readily available for the small and big boater alike. Millions of Pacific salmon are stocked each year into the Great Lakes and this is when the mature salmon will begin staging off the tributary mouths.

Since the appetites of these lunker salmon have diminished, fishing can be as unpredictable as the weather. It's an excellent time to catch that trophy fish you've always wanted on the wall at home, because catching one of these monsters isn't the true test of angling proficiency this time of year. The real test comes from fishing consistency.

For early fall salmon fishing, you're dealing with three basic methods for success. Dodgers, spoons or J-plugs are the main techniques that work when these salmon come to the streams where they were stocked. Boat speed and lead length are the two keys that contribute most heavily to success.

If working dodgers, vary your speed from .8 to 1.8 mph. If you're in a situation where you can't seem to slow your speed to where the fish will hit, you might want to consider extending your leads and running lazy S-turn trolls. Vary your leads until you find what the fish want. There is no set rule. Fish can be taken off dodgers 80 feet back behind the downrigger ball. On the other hand, salmon can be taken as close as 8 feet off the ball with J-plugs. It just depends upon conditions.

If fish are close to shore, start with J-plugs off the bottom and move out deeper as sunlight increases, but switch over to dodgers on the bottom if action slows. Although J-plugs are generally run fast, you may want to slow your presentation down and stack dodgers or spoons around them to take advantages of the attraction capabilities of the dodgers ...

Dealing with this time period is not always an easy proposition. They could be in front of the piers or they could be out in much deeper water. That's one of the reasons why it's a good idea to run J-plugs and magnum spoons at a faster clip—2½ to 3½ mph. It allows more water to be covered and locate the fish before fine-tuning a presentation.

Once a fish school is located, systematically work it until you find what the salmon want: Vary the speed, running glow, black and silver colors. Leads will also vary, but dodgers start around 10 feet back behind the downrigger ball. Gradually extend those leads until you find something that works.

Run a few Dipsy Divers, too. If you start catching fish on them, you'll know to extend your leads if fish are ball shy. Also run Dipsy Divers shallow. Let out 35 to 40 feet from your reel, put the diving plane on the third setting and run the lure closer to the surface. This will only put your bait about 10 feet down, but away from the boat.

To help insure better success, use a sharp hook point. They're essential to more consistent fishing. When the fish start to stage off the tributary mouths, use 00-size dodgers of varying leads, dropping them to varying depths. That's where the kings will be. If fishing shallow, leads may stretch to 30 feet. If running deeper, leads only need to be about 6 to 10 feet back.

Baits and colors vary with conditions, too. Any type of glow squid off dodgers will usually produce fish. Dodger color may vary from day to day, but whatever you do, try to keep the same colors within your sets on each side of the boat—don't mix and match. And when something starts working for you, don't be afraid to run everything the same. You can also stack spoons around the dodgers to simulate baitfish, and use the attractive qualities of the dodger to your advantage. Remember, you're trying to get fall fish mad at your lures, because they're not feeding as much, if at all.

Trolling a J-Plug, and paying attention to detail, handsomely rewarded NAFC Charter Member Monte Kennedy who caught this 34-pound chinook in 60 feet of Lake Ontario's water.

Paying attention to detail is always an important key to fishing success. Doing that, and listening to helpful tips increases your fishing proficiency in the fall more consistently. Don't be afraid to try new things; however, the old stand-bys are usually hard to beat.

Here's a lake-by-lake scenario for the types of trolling tactics that seem to work:

Lake Ontario
If you're using planer boards or downriggers, run your lures as far back as you can get away with. If you run them too far back, you'll have less hook-setting power and less action on your spoons. Bigger spring kings have a tendency to like water under them, so you might be trolling in 50 to 60 feet of water. Look for a temperature break 5 to 25 feet down.

Big, deep-running body baits are used when flatlining. One pattern that has worked in the past is stacking spoons: one spoon 15 feet directly off the cannonball; another lure just above it about 30 feet back. When doing this, run all the same color. Kings that are cannonball-shy will take the top lure.

Trolling For Salmon

Another pattern that works well is used by captain Vince Pierleoni of Oak Orchard—running downrigger "sets" to simulate a baitfish school. Lures are staggered in 5-foot increments off two downriggers at varying levels. Pierleoni thinks that the Yeck spoons work best for him in the spring (once again, confidence by the angler) because it's good in current, and more speed-forgiving than some other spoons.

Charter captain Bob Koperski of Wilson, New York, capitalizes on both coho and chinook fishing in the spring, summer and fall. If for some reason he can't locate fish close to shore right away, he's not afraid to run to where there are fish. Trolling along the shoreline with both planer boards and flatlining, he will do excellent on coho, as well as mixed bag for other salmonids. Stickbaits work well, concentrating on visual-type fishing—watching his water temperature and looking for a debris line. "Be aware of what the water is doing, and what the wind is doing to the water," he says.

Koperski also has this rule on leads: "If I'm fishing above 40 feet, I'll use medium-long leads. If I'm below 40 feet, I'll use short to medium leads. However, I never run leads longer than I have to."

When tackling kings, anglers may need to head out to 100 feet of water before they find the right school they're looking for. On the average, work about 30 feet down, staggering leads until the right combination shows up. Boat speed should be between 2 and 2.6 mph. Primary colors should be black in front with white in back; green; chartreuse; and silver to start off. Spoons are preferred in the spring because their percentage of hookups tends to be better. Spoons in the 3-inch magnum size are what they run the most—Pirates, Southports, Northern Kings. The main reason why they'll make that extra run for kings is simple: a 15-pound average; fish between 20 and 30 pounds are common occurrences in the spring. In summer, they're putting on some bulk, with a 22- to 25-pound average for mature fish come fall.

Charter captain John DeLorenzo of Niagara Falls is another guide who likes to run where the best king fishing is. He says that it's usually easier to stack rods than to use sliders in shallower depths. Proper instrumentation is important for him, for a number of reasons. He keys on temperature breaks. Once located, he utilizes a Loran-C to stay on the fish. A school of fish might only be 100 feet across, so being able to maintain that location is important—helping him put more fish in the boat than any other piece of equipment.

Head for deep water, and fish the top 50 to 70 feet along thermal breaks with an "M" or "W" pattern. Charter captain Jeremiah Heffernan will locate bait pods over deep water, and start trolling there. If there's baitfish, salmon won't be far away.

"By running an 'M' or 'W' pattern with my downriggers," he said, "I can take salmon down deep, but pick up steelhead up high. Any type of a large temperature break will normally hold fish. Work them hard to pick up both chinook and coho."

One popular summer technique is using a dodger/squid or dodger/fly. Slow trolling is necessary to achieve the right action. This same technique will carry into fall, along with body baits like J-Plugs or Silver Hordes trolled along the bottom. Since fall fish really aren't feeding, use a lure that's mean and ugly—to make these fish mad.

Lake Erie

Planer boards distributing orange and chartreuse stick or body baits will tend to outproduce spoons on these waters. Charter captain Pete Alex, from Erie, Pennsylvania, will run his plugs just 5 feet off the boards, or just 20 feet off the boat with flatlines.

Alex will fish the "mountain" just outside the harbor at Erie, Pennsylvania, targeting cohos laying on the ledge of the most severe drop-off in the area. Dodgers leading either squid or flies, or body baits, work well trolling the bottom.

Lake Huron

Captain Terry Promowicz of Flint, Michigan, starts the second week of April, with fishing taking place from Port Huron to Port Austin. He'll typically run high lines, shallow divers and downriggers from the surface to 30 feet down, depending on the area. Two- and 3-year-old fish will make up most of your catch as you troll shallower water for a mixed bag of fish. A mixture of kings, cohos, Atlantics and triploid fish can all be caught.

Since fish are active in the spring, you can keep your speed from 1.7 to 2.3 mph, depending on what you're pulling and how long of leads you're running.

Off the downriggers, Promowicz prefers 3- to 8-foot leads off the cannon balls when trolling medium-weight spoons. If there's loads of natural bait on hand, look for warm runs to draw them in. Work the shoreline in and out. If there isn't a lot of bait, go with a slower movement and longer leads to entice fish. Divers, drop weights and planer boards all work well in taking fish.

Fish closer to the bottom. Try trolling larger spoons deep, with smaller, lighter spoons on stackers above the lower baits. Fish like this until August, with your standard complement of divers, lead core, drop weights and the like. Body baits and dodger fishing will take over at this point on staging kings.

Lake Michigan

Boat fishermen will utilize artificial enticements, as well as live bait in the form of smelt and alewives. Charter captain Russ Clark of St. Joseph says that the top lures for him include small body baits (such as Hot 'N Tots), and smaller-sized spoons in chartreuse, yellow, green, red, orange or blue, depending on the day ... and the fish.

One favorite pattern of Clark's is locating a sandbar and fishing the deeper troughs, running planer boards on either side of the bar. He also has a tendency to run planer boards extremely close to shore when many of his tried-and-true methods aren't working satisfactorily in the lake.

Big, mature salmon averaging 10 to 15 pounds are boated each spring using many of the same methods that have already been outlined for early-season action.

When fishing early in the year in clear water under clear skies, use long leads. Probably 90 percent of your fishing tactics will involve the use of spoons: Yeck magnums in lemon lime, egg shell or chartreuse. To darken them, add a ladder- or tiger-back pattern to the spoon's back.

Follow your surface temperature meter. Small secluded pockets with small temperature differences (sometimes as small as one degree), are the key to finding fish, and are the more consistent catches.

Trolling speed is important, too. Every boat is calibrated

This spoon selection is popular on the Great Lakes. These spoons are generally effective because they imitate baitfish that may be in the area. Several have reflective strips on them for greater attraction.

differently, so be aware that a "2" on one boat might not be the same as a "2" on another vessel. Keep your speed between 1.9 and 2.5 on a knot meter.

Fish with what you feel most comfortable with. Gain confidence in something you're doing, and you'll catch fish.

Knowing the size of baitfish in your area will help you know what to offer the fish. Try to keep consistent.

One of the hot baits is a spoon with red slashes across a laser-yellow stripe, simulating a perch. Cut the wings off a ladder-back and add red eyes. It really does work!

Lake Superior

For cohos, Maki will have customers toss ¼- to ¾-ounce leadhead jigs tipped with a piece of cut bait while drifting along the shoreline. Trolling for chinook salmon is also an option, pulling spoons or body baits under the boat with downriggers. He'll troll out to 70-foot depths, keeping his lures 30 to 50 feet down. Speed in the spring varies from 1.5 to 2.5 mph due to the cold water. Don't be surprised to see a constant 38- or 39-degree temperature in the early spring.

Trolling For Salmon

In the fall, it's all downrigger fishing for salmon. Speed increases due to warmer water temperatures, sometimes up to 3.5 mph. Once again, concentrate on river inlets.

Trolling For Landlocked Salmon

The landlocked Atlantic salmon of eastern North America eagerly pursue a fast-moving lure, particularly if it resembles a baitfish. A variety of shiny wobblers, either smooth or crinkle finish, work well. However, the most effective lures are minnow imitation plugs. In selecting a wobbler, insist on those with an optimum action at a high-trolling speed. The action on most minnow imitation plugs must be slightly modified to run at faster than normal speeds. (It's basically a trial-and-error process to find just the right angle to bend the wire loop.)

During the first part of the season, the landlocked salmon are usually close to the surface and stay there until about a week after the smelt runs are finished. After that, they follow the smelt schools to deeper, cooler water as summer progresses. One effective trolling technique is to run the lure right in the tail-end of the turbulence created by the outboard motor. Landlocked salmon seem to have learned that propellers occasionally injure baitfish, which then become easy prey.

The other extreme, used primarily during the early season, is to troll an extremely long line. The reasoning behind this technique is that the boat tends to spook the fish in its path, leaving a channel of barren water behind it. However, this channel gradually closes once more when the fish return to normal activity. Between 80 and 100 yards of line usually seems to do the trick. Again, minnow imitation plugs and wobblers provide good results.

Streamer Flies

Another effective technique is to troll streamer flies—primarily patterns such as Magog Smelt, Nine Three, Green Ghost and Black Ghost. Tandem dressings are preferred since they provide a larger profile when trolled. When trolling with fly-fishing gear, use a full sinking line—for spring fishing, a normal sinking line completely extended will take the fly down about 8 feet to the most productive level. Spinning gear with about 8-pound-test monofilament can also be used to troll these streamers; during the first month after ice out, attach a couple of split shots to take the offering down to the fish. Later in the season, you'll need more sophisticated methods to reach the salmon in deeper water.

During early season, you'll find the landlocked salmon close to shore, especially in stream vicinities where smelt spawn. Often, during the first few weeks after ice-out, boats trolling so close to shore that the rodtips almost touch the shoreline branches do the most business. By the beginning of June, through most of their southern range, the landlocked salmon have gone deep. The best way to find them is to locate the smelt schools and troll back and forth through them, preferably with the lure just below the bottom of the school.

The mistake most inexperienced landlocked salmon fishermen make is trying to strike the fish the instant they feel a hit. Rather than striking at the bait, landlocked salmon prefer to stun or maim prey, then come back to leisurely pick up the minnow. When the angler feels a hit, the proper reaction is to drop the rodtip and wait for the fish to come back to pick up the offering. If no hit is forthcoming within a minute or two, try teasing the fish by jerking on the line to imitate a crippled baitfish. It's usually more than a landlocked salmon can bear.

=17=

Mooching And Motor Mooching

West Coast salmon fishermen have an effective method of angling that uses light tackle and is a hands-on direct connection to biting fish. It quickens heartbeats from the first delicate nibbles to the pounding and surging of reel-straining runs. "Mooching" may have collected more silvery fish scales on boat bottoms and in fish boxes than any other Western salmon technique. It works especially well from Tillamook Bay, Oregon, to the inlets of upper Alaska, in most areas where salmon continue to feed through saltwater into brackish water and anywhere freshwater curtains extend over the brine toward the Pacific.

Simplicity is the keyword to mooching. With motors shut down, even beginners can sink hooks into cavorting coho or ponderous chinook while taking a leisurely free drift furnished by tide, current or wind and dangling herring-laden hooks below. Veteran salmon anglers who keep fishing logbooks refine the tactic further. On certain days, stages of tide, hours of day and moon phases, they will fish a particular-sized herring "X" feet deep over favorite spots.

Mooching rods usually are the 8- to 11-foot rods described in Chapter 4, and uniformly have sensitive tips, gradual strength development in mid-spine and enough beef in their butt sections to persuade an exhausted salmon into a waiting net. Most Westerners will opt for a sturdy, large-capacity, levelwind reel filled with line from 10-pound test up to

This 32-pound chinook salmon smacked a Mooch-A-Jig fished off a point in the Strait of Juan de Fuca in Washington state.

Mooching And Motor Mooching 211

These salmon fell for this herring aid in a big way. Trollers often make their presentations attractive by using a herring aid which makes the bait look more realistic.

30-pound monofilament. In British Columbia, centre-pin reels are preferred and in some areas, big saltwater spinning reels are considered just fine for mooching.

Mooching leads resemble small, slightly flattened bananas with a bead-chain swivel at one end and a barrel swivel at the other. Most salmon anglers swear by a standard sinker's normal lead color, but a few scrape the sinkers with a knife blade to leave shiny, attractive streaks. Other fishermen choose painted red, orange, pink, lime, fluorescent orange or chartreuse mooching sinkers to add more invitation to their rigs.

Note that sinker swivels, intended to reduce line and leader twist, are different lengths, short and long. You can generate some lively and heated debates when asking two side-by-side fishermen which end is up and which down! If you tie your

Using a centre-pin reel and a long trolling rod, this angler was able to bring in a matched pair of bright sockeye salmon. These fish were taken in British Columbia.

Mooching And Motor Mooching

Mooching Angles

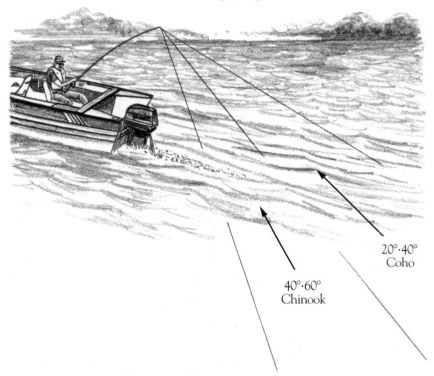

20°-40°
Coho

40°-60°
Chinook

An easy rule of thumb for determining proper mooching sinker weights is calculating the angle between the line and the water. Change sinkers until the angle matches the species that is being sought.

main line to the single swivel, however, and leader to the bead chain end, you should have fewer twisted leaders.

Many salmon anglers use pre-tied, inexpensive 5- to 7-foot mooching leaders, carrying one to two snelled hooks in sizes 1/0 to 4/0. Some veteran anglers prefer to tie their own leaders, which is easily done. Commonly, the upper hook of two-hook leaders will be one size larger than the trailing hook (4/0 and 3/0, 3/0 and 2/0, for example).

Two styles of salmon leaders are used. Fixed tie, where the hooks cannot move, is standard. A sliding-tie leader allows the upper hook to move slightly so an angler can achieve a slight bend in his herring that satisfies him with a "just right" roll and spin in the water. However, with sliding tie leaders, large salmon barbed only by the upper hook may fight long and hard, fraying and finally parting the leader where the sliding tie moves on the line. This can cause the loss of a large fish.

Experienced salmon fishermen know chinook prefer to have the bait rotate slowly; a slightly faster spin appeals to coho salmon. Accordingly, anglers rig the baitfish to get the highest rate of bite selectivity from the species for which they are angling. (The bait section discusses whole herring, cut-plug herring, fillet strip herring preparation and use of herring aids, all of which affect that critical spin timing.)

Whether fishing with a depthfinder that indicates fish, on charters where the skipper or mate advises correct fishing depths or when tackling well-known, favorite rips or currents, putting your mooching gear into the water slowly and smoothly is the next vital step. Your line and leader must go down without tangling to spark a salmon's interest.

"Counting Out"

Save your sympathy pangs for any mooching angler you see slowly pulling line from his reel. He's generally not removing a backlash; instead, he is "counting out" a predetermined number of 2-foot "pulls" of monofilament calculated to put his herring right in front of and just above a salmon's nose.

The distance from your reel's levelwind guide to your salmon rod's first guide is slightly over 2 feet, which allows you to grasp the mono between thumb and forefinger and repeatedly pull it from reel to first guide until a desired length of line is let out. This studied procedure normally ensures your sinker won't rotate, creating a bird's nest of line and leader.

Another good method of letting out monofilament is to measure line released when free-spooling from one side of a reel to the other. Called a "turn," this should feed 5 to 8 feet of line from most saltwater levelwind reels. If you restrain the line going out by pressing your thumb lightly on the reel spool, so the pull of bait, sinker and line is slow and steady, you'll have fewer tangles.

How much line you let out depends on the salmon species you are after and the depth at which you know or suspect they are finning. A couple different "mooching line angles" will help you. Trial-and-error have shown that your bait's movement is most acceptable to chinook when the angle of your

Mooching And Motor Mooching   215

Mooching paid off for NAFC Member Ken Smith of Clovis, California, while fishing for salmon in Monterey Bay in July. His reward was this nice 42-pound king salmon.

monofilament is between 40 and 60 degrees off horizontal from rodtip to water. Coho strike better on the spinning action accomplished when your line angle is between 20 and 40 degrees to the surface.

Achieving this angle means changing your bait's speed through the water and its rotation for the desired species, resulting in optimum fishing. Getting the proper angle without using your motor is as simple as changing sinker weights until the line angle falls within the parameters you want.

Motor Mooching

"Motor mooching" sometimes produces strikes when salmon are picky about gumming a herring presented with standard mooching. To generate a little more "pizzazz," try running your outboard at a slow speed for a short distance, then popping the shift lever into idle for a few minutes, back to low, and then to idle again. What you are doing is speeding your herring's motion through the water while causing it to rise a bit toward the surface when the boat is in low gear. Idling slows the bait, causing it to drop back down. You are fluctuating both rotation of the herring and the level at which different and perhaps more salmon can spot it.

Every fisherman enjoys the smashing strike of a "suicide salmon" and many fish do solidly hook themselves on the first bite. Experienced salmon anglers know they'll catch their limit more often by showing a little patience when the first, delicate nibbles dip their rodtips.

Salmon often seize a baitfish, bite it once or twice, and then let go. They will come back, determined to put a little heftier hurt on it. Finally, ready to eat, the salmon takes the bait firmly in its mouth and begins swimming off. Your rod bows in the middle and begins to pump in tune with the fish's tail movements. That's the time to come back smoothly on your rod to set the hook.

Setting the hook on a salmon is not done as you would sock it to a steelhead or a large trout. Just raising your rod firmly is enough to put the hook point deep into a salmon's mouth and, when a spiked fish cuts in its afterburners on the first run, the barb will be solidly embedded. If you're fishing with a barbless hook, as required in some salmon areas, you'll find that it, too, will strike home, and you only have to avoid slack in your monofilament to prevent the fish from shaking the hook.

18

Pier Fishing Tactics

Literally millions of sportfishing enthusiasts in the United States confine all their angling activities to the shore, for whatever reason. The next best thing to boat fishing, then, is to take advantage of the many piers, break walls and jetties that extend out into the water—especially in the Great Lakes Basin.

Pier fishing for salmon has become an art, employing a variety of techniques at different times of the year to entice the mighty salmon into hitting your offering. The best thing about pier fishing is that it's easy to learn, whether it's with artificial or live bait.

Generally speaking, piers, break walls and jetties are situated in areas that are naturals for attracting fish. These areas include river and creek mouths, as well as entrances to harbors. In the springtime, warmer waters will attract baitfish, in addition to predator fish like salmon. In the fall, these are the areas where salmon plants were made, so mature fish will be returning to spawn.

Wind and weather also dictate how consistent you can be off the piers. Wind blowing into shore during the spring can have a positive effect by pushing warmer water from other areas toward you. This, in turn, will bring in baitfish and salmon in search of warmer water temperatures.

In the summer, the reverse is true. Offshore breezes can push warmer waters out away from the piers, and actually bring

You don't have to be in a boat to catch nice salmon like this one taken by a Great Lakes pier fisherman. Early-spring and late-fall are good times to fish from shore.

Pier Fishing Tactics

colder water in close to shore. Although not a common occurrence, this can provide decent close-in shore fishing for salmonids at a time when shore anglers are normally restricted to warm-water fish species.

Piers, break walls and jetties, by their very nature, are natural fish attractants, serving as important structure that fish can adapt to—both baitfish and the prey who gorge themselves on that bait.

Pier fishing involves daily patterns established through fish migrations. Early in the morning, fish will have a tendency to be closer to the shoreline. As the morning progresses, fish gradually will move out to deeper water. At least, most of them will. If you want to play the percentages, move with the larger fish schools.

Pier casters should concentrate their efforts during early morning and evening, especially on clear, sunny days. There will be more consistent action throughout the day if skies are overcast.

Weather also helps you decide what color might be most effective for you when tossing artificials to finicky salmon. For example, overcast days might dictate the use of black spoons with gold tape. Chartreuse will work well if the water is slightly off-color from seasonal runoff. Silver and any color combination might turn fish in the spring when fish are just starting to become active again. Cohos are your most likely target among Great Lakes salmon options in the spring; both coho and chinook are good in the fall.

Since most of your fishing takes place on or near the bottom, ¼- or ½-ounce spoons and spinners are the most popular hardware to cast. Carefully select a site on the pier, and start to cast, fanning out in all directions. Look for places that may hold fish, such as underwater structure (i.e., rock piles and old piers, mud lines, current rips or back eddies).

When retrieving your lure, give it an erratic motion. Adjust your retrieval speed from slow to medium to fast. Stop your retrieve for a second and start back up again. Move your rodtip from side to side, or up and down, varying speed, direction and your overall presentation. More often than not, it's these erratic inconsistencies that trigger a fish to hit.

Casting large, deep-diving stickbaits, in addition to jigs

Bait Set-ups For Pier Fishing

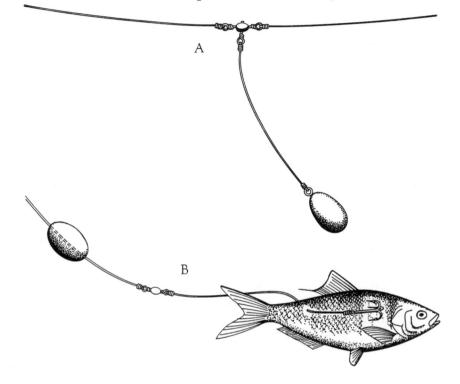

These rigs are popular with pier fishermen. While some use artificials with the three-way rig (A), others swear by live bait which can be used on that rig or with the live bait rig (B).

tipped with bait (such as smelt and alewives), has also worked well to influence fish strikes. Small body baits will work during certain times of the year.

Although artificials produce fish, old pier-fishing diehards will still insist that the only way to go is with live (or dead) bait. Smelt and alewives are always popular enticements, as are worms, leeches, gizzard shad and minnows.

If you don't believe that live bait fishing can be effective on salmon, just ask William Ryan of Auburn, New York. The veteran pier-and-shore fisherman has been able to consistently catch fish in the spring and fall—and have a good time doing it.

Ryan prefers using live alewives whenever possible. In the spring, he'll use an ultra-light rod with extremely small homemade jigs and flies (too small to cast) to catch alewives along the piers. These live fish are then threaded with an English-type hook and attached with 1 to 2½ feet of 12-pound-test leader line, with lead length dependent upon personal preference. This connects to a swivel, with a sliding sinker just above the swivel, completing the rig.

For springtime fishing, cohos will be the primary target, with chinooks preferring slightly deeper waters. You'll also pick up quite a few trout in the process. In the Empire State/Lake Ontario Trout and Salmon Derby, the largest of its kind in the U.S. with more than 13,000 participants, Ryan beat out the thousands of boats trolling the waters of the big lake by pier-fishing with live alewives. His catch of a 25-pound-plus brown trout earned him a cash prize package of nearly $20,000! On the day he caught the big fish, he had reeled in seven fish over 12 pounds—all on live bait off the pier.

In the fall, this same technique works for staging coho and chinook salmon at creek and river mouths, either from shore or off the piers. These one-time boat fishermen found that there were many advantages to live-bait pier and shore fishing. Weather wasn't an important factor pertaining to getting out on the water. It was also much more comfortable.

Once they decided the piers were the way to go, they began casting spoons. And, although they caught fish, they decided to experiment with live-bait fishing, after reading an article in a major magazine.

"We thought it made more sense to live-bait fish, because it allowed us to keep our baits in the water for a longer period of time," said Ryan. "We started out with big pike shiners, and we caught a few fish, but things really started to happen for us when we went to live alewives. In the fall, we fish two poles each, giving us plenty of opportunity. There are many days we out-fish the boat trollers."

Ryan thinks that the naturally-aggressive nature of the alewife, along with a putrid odor that goes along with this prime forage helps to attract salmon into hitting in the fall—when these fish are no longer eating.

It's necessary to keep an open bail with salmon, because of the tremendous hits that occur sometimes. Ryan often will place a quarter on the line as a hit signal; at other times, he'll use a rubber band. Because alewives are very active in the water, some resistance is needed to help keep them from stripping line from the open bail. By taking a rubber band and placing it just above the reel (actually, after taking the reel off to slide it up the rod), you can thread the line through and on up through the guides. The rubber band will create enough tension to stop your bait, but not a powerful salmon. This is important because you could lose your whole fishing outfit if you're not careful.

Probably, the single most important bait to use for salmon, especially in the fall, is a big glob of fresh egg skein or carefully-tied egg sacks. (Preparation of egg skeins and loose eggs for use as bait is covered in Chapter 12.)

While the fresh salmon eggs will work—both still in the skein and tied up in egg sacks—many pier fishermen prefer to doctor their eggs with prepackaged fish egg cures to make them even more appealing to the fish, and to preserve them better.

These can be worked along the bottom with a three-way rig or another such sinker system. One trick is to put small Styrofoam balls in the sack as an attractant and to give the sack more buoyancy. Slip bobbers are also used heavily by veteran pier-casters.

Whatever you do, don't forget a long-handled fishnet so you can haul your catch up from the water. With fall fish tipping the scales at more than 30 pounds (in some instances), these fish command respect if you intend to fully complete your battle. Good luck!

19

Jigging For Kings And Cohos

J igging for salmon is a technique often overlooked by fishermen who probably don't give it the respect it deserves. However, whenever the fish stack for whatever reason, it may be the most viable way of inducing strikes from salmon that may not be in the mood to take other presentations. In this chapter, we take a look at two variations of the jigging theme—deep-water jigging and light-tackle presentations.

Deep Jigging

The technique that probably has the smallest following, but can very well be the most productive and exciting—and the greatest potential for experimentation, proving extremely effective at catching salmon during the spring, summer and fall—is deep jigging.

The approach is simple. Send a heavy spoon or jig into the area you've identified as holding fish, be it underwater structure or some sort of thermal pocket or preferred temperature zone. Let your line out until you've reached your target, and then start to work your bait in an up-and-down fashion. You might raise your rod a half a foot; you might lift it the entire length of the rod. You might jerk the rod quickly, or do a gradual lift. Vary your jigging strokes continually to create that all-important, erratic action.

It's on the downward fall of your lure—giving it the

This nice, 28-pound chinook hit a No. 4 Nordic Glo-Green jig while these anglers were jigging on the Columbia River in the Pacific Northwest.

Jigging For Kings And Cohos

appearance of a struggling or dying baitfish—when strikes will normally occur. As your lure falls back to the bottom, any peculiar action or hesitation of the line, as it descends, is cause for setting the hook. Or, if no hesitation was noticed, and you can feel tension at the end of your rod—set the hook! You have to react quickly. The initial strikes are not easily detected.

When jigging, it's important to allow for a slight pause as the lure settles back down. One to two seconds should suffice, but it should be a noticeable stop. Vary your stop times.

Pat Barber of Niagara Falls is one salmon angler who prefers jigging for salmon, especially in the springtime when fish are concentrated. "In April and early May, salmon are still in large schools and can be jigged up relatively easy," said Barber, a member of the "Killer B's" fishing team. "Areas such as the mouth of the Niagara River are excellent locations to experiment with deep-jigging techniques because there are so many fish present. All the necessary ingredients to hold fish—bottom structure, current and thermal structure—are present in the spring. We'll work the drop-offs for coho and chinook, and pick up bonus trout in the process."

Barber likes to use a three-way swivel and tie-off a heavy spoon 18 inches to 2 feet down. Off a second eye, he ties on a jig with a twister tail. It could be a minnow, or chunk of smelt or alewife, too. When working this up and down across bottom structure, especially over deep-sloping ledges, he takes fish on both baits.

Depending on the depth you're jigging, color selection can be very important. The deeper you go, the greater attention to detail must be paid. Colors will change at varying depths.

No matter where or when you're fishing, it's important to have good electronics to locate bottom structure holding fish. Temperature probes are essential to identify preferred water levels for salmon. For coho and chinook, 55 degrees is an optimum temperature. Their active range will stretch from 44 to 58 degrees on the average, although these fish have been known to work outside the norm—especially in the fall.

Heavy spoons imitating the shape and size of baitfish peculiar to that area is one of the more popular approaches. Heavy jigs tipped with twister tails, rubber worms or pork rind have taken their fair share of fish. Tipping those same jigs with the actual baitfish—such as smelt and alewives in the Great Lakes—will also work jigging wonders.

Jigging has become an important part of some charter fishing services, too. One case in point is Jim Maki's operation out of Marquette, Michigan, on Lake Superior. He uses the jigging concept throughout the season, finding it a most effective method for putting fish into the boat ... and keeping people happy.

In the springtime, he jigs the south shore of the lake in search of battling coho. Areas off power plants whose warm-water discharges are excellent man-made fish attractors are good spots in the early season. Maki prefers to toss ¼- to ¾-ounce leadhead jigs tipped with a piece of cut bait, drifting and casting over structure. He likes to keep the jig fairly close to the bottom, but he does find fish suspended off the bottom on occasion.

Come summer, he works around the big reef area 40 miles from his home port, with Standard Rock his intended target. Here, again, a similar jigging technique is used, working 1-ounce leadhead jigs at the end of 10-pound-test dacron line and 20 feet of 8-pound-test monofilament as a leader. He prefers to use a 7-foot, medium-action graphite rod with open-faced reels when jigging over structure. Although most of his catch this time of year consists of lake trout (his biggest so far has been 33 pounds, with 20-plus pounders relatively common), he will pick up bonus salmon while fishing this area.

While the preferred jigging bait involves the actual forage from the Great Lakes, primarily smelt and alewives, either still alive, preserved, or cut, strides are being made with the use of artificial baits made from the same protein-based food and bait by-products that occur naturally. Experimentation is still occurring in the Great Lakes as to how these baits will fare. At a time when there's plenty of concern over the main forage base of the Great Lakes, this might be a viable option for sportfishermen—especially if you can catch just as many, if not more, on these artificial baits.

Using these same techniques at night has led to respectable success in the Great Lakes. Boats are equipped with powerful lights which attract baitfish under the drifting boat. Once baitfish show up, it won't be long before the salmon start

For serious jigging, anglers usually choose a small boat which is more maneuverable in river channels and creates less disturbance when jigging for salmon.

to make their way onto the scene. Using your electronics to identify proper depths and fish locations, you can then try to jig effectively with spoons or live bait. If you've got a good graph, you can even watch your bait working up and down in the fish zone.

Deep-jigging rods are generally shorter and stiffer, giving you more power and better control in your motion. Proper line class is important. If you normally fish with 10-pound test, bump it up to 12-pound for jigging. Be sure your drag is set light, too, for when a salmon hits. If your drag is set tight, you've just lost some more hardware—and another battle with a salmon.

Light-Tackle Jigging

Wherever you find salmon "stacking"—off river mouths, in inlets, straits, sounds, bays, estuaries, lakes and reservoirs—you can have excellent light-tackle sport by jigging for them. These spots where numbers of salmon linger before final dashes into spawning rivers are often carpeted or layered with hundreds of fish so peckish about taking bait and standard lures that fishermen label them "lockjaw" fish.

Of course, they can be caught—by a switch in tackle and tactics. It's time to get out a heavy-duty bass flippin' or popping rod—or any medium-weight casting rod that measures 6½ to 8 feet—load a high-quality, large-capacity levelwind reel with 8- to 12-pound-test mono, grab a handful of jigs and jigging spoons and head your boat for the hotspot!

A depth locator or fishfinder is critical, because you must know where salmon schools are located and their level in the water. Once you have pinpointed a school, the key to good jigging catches is to free-spool your jig or spoon down to them, crank the reel into gear and dance the lure a foot or two above all those watching eyeballs.

The most productive jigging stroke is to raise your rodtip several feet smoothly, then drop the tip to follow the line down just fast enough to feel the lure's weight. It takes a little practice, but shouldn't be too long before you can tell when a coho or chinook salmon grabs the descending lure. Since most takes occur as the lure dips and sinks, any cessation of lure weight means it is time to strike.

Another kind of hookup often enjoyed by light-tackle salmon jiggers is when a fisherman intends to raise his rod for the upstroke and finds he can't budge it, or that a strong, pulsating and swiftly accelerating finny critter on the other end is already smoking line from under his thumb!

Your best salmon jigging hours are from gray daylight for about three to four hours or until the sun fully hits the water, and again for the last hour or two before dark. Salmon move higher in the water in low-light levels and fin deeper when the sun is bright.

Half the fun is perfecting your technique, and altering your approach in order to catch more fish. Jigging isn't just for ice fishing or for taking warm-water fish species anymore. Try it on salmon, too. You might be pleasantly surprised.

=20=

Inland, Coastal Special Techniques

Apfor-to-June anglers fishing long and light rods in the Campbell River area of Discovery Passage (inshore side of Vancouver Island, B.C.) for winter "spring" chinook, weighing 25 pounds or more, use special rigging enhancing the fighting abilities of this great fish. These fish "winter over" in local waters and, in spring, pursue herring schools by herding them against Quadra Island while foraging heavily on the baitfish.

Rods most commonly used here are 10 to 11½ feet long, equipped with smooth-operating, levelwind, starwheel drag reels or high quality centre-pin reels, 10-pound-test main line, ⅜-ounce to ⅝-ounce bead chain keel sinkers and 8-pound monofilament leaders. The leaders terminate in two relatively small hooks when considering the size of the quarry—a No. 1 single salmon hook followed by a No. 8 treble hook.

Live herring are preferred winter "spring" salmon baits and often are jigged or "raked" from the same waters you will fish. Ironically, the salmon you want to catch may help you take your bait herring. Most herring are jigged from the deep waters brushing against Quadra Island, their spring spawning area. Chinook herd herring against the shore of Quadra, concentrating thousands of baitfish in a moving smorgasbord.

Herring Rigs And Rakes
The herring jigging rig is a short, stout rod, sturdy reel and

230   Complete Angler's Library

This 63-pound, sea-run chinook is a good example of the fish that congregate around Vancouver Island, British Columbia, and forage heavily on herring. This youngster caught this monster in the Gold River.

Inland, Coastal Special Techniques

heavy monofilament carrying a sinker at the bottom and five to seven small, bushy bucktail jigs spaced above the sinker on short leaders projecting in all directions. This rig is cast to a herring school, which still feeds on the run even while under predator attack. And, several baitfish are lightly struck before retrieving.

Herring "rakes" are long wood or fiberglass poles, the last 3 feet or so ending in a flat piece of metal having many thin, long and sharp up-slanted needles on either side. This is plunged into a herring school and artfully swept up and into the boat with wriggling herring lightly pinned by the needles. Sounds simple, but it takes skill and practice.

Baitfish are kept alive in a large, plastic dishpan, halfway filled with often-changed saltwater. With little damage from jigging or raking, these herring are active, energetic baits.

Hook a herring through the nose crosswise, just in front of the eyes, with the No. 1 hook and pin the trailing treble hook to its flank. The bait is trolled near the hurrying and harried schools of herring besieged by chinook salmon. From 26 to 40 2-foot pulls of line off the reel generally will allow the baitfish to fall into harm's way of a feeding salmon.

Because of the light line, it is essential not to answer the slow tapping and waited-for long pull of a salmon's bite with a sharp strike. Instead, raise your rodtip high and nudge hook barbs home with a couple wrist movements only. Then, the fun begins!

A Little Dab'll Do You

One of the tiny tricks that will add extra fish to a salmon troller's catches, or even save him from a fishless day, is to "sweeten" a dodger/flasher, two-hook leader and artificial lure setup with a small triangle of baitfish flesh. It's quick and easy to cut these productive triangles from herring.

Take a fresh herring or thaw out a 6- to 8-inch bait from a commercial package and fillet one side from behind the gills to the tail. Cut right through rib bones and leave the skin on. Next, slice half a dozen triangles from the fillet and barb one on the upper hook of a plastic squid, flashtail or hoochie rig by inserting the hook barb through the tidbit about ⅜ of an inch from the tip of the narrowest point.

Triangled Herring Presentation

With a triangle herring presentation (top), a herring fillet triangle is tipped on the leading hook, and the squid and weight are allowed to slide down to it. A herring fillet can be quickly cut into this bait form, as indicated below.

Salmon will answer the siren call of dinner on the table and gladly chomp this rig while often ignoring an identical setup fished without the tasty addition. This works extremely well in inshore waters rife with dog sharks or mud sharks that gobble regularly mooched herring baits, but generally snub or can't grab trolled artificials. Their weak eyes, slower speed and less efficient sense of smell keeps them off the hook that now better attracts salmon.

Jealousy Works Wonders

Anyone who has ever watched small fish in an aquarium or a pond knows about the competition that goes on when one fish finds a morsel too big for it to immediately swallow. The possessor is chased and harassed by other eager eaters trying to snatch the food away. Put this to work for you wherever a bunch of salmon have an opportunity to indulge in some petty greediness and you'll boost your catches.

Always pack some silver/gray plastic squid imitations with you when mooching or trolling big, deep salt or brackish salmon areas and use 'em to create a little envy and appetite. Clip or pierce the look-alike squid at its tip so your leader can be slid through it before tying it to sinker or dodger. Slide the squid down the leader atop a whole herring and spread its legs over the head of the baitfish as though it were being carried off.

Any self-respecting salmon is not going to let the "little guy in his neighborhood" take off with such a succulent mouthful without trying to take it away ... and eating the impudent squirt in the process. Strike!

Never Say "Never"

"Sportfishermen won't catch any, or very many sockeye salmon," oldtimers continued to tell West Coast salmon anglers until the 1960s. They knew sockeye ignored most baits because they fed on plankton and other tiny saltwater organisms ... and the oldtimers were correct for a long time. Slowly, and then more and more quickly, these savants were compelled to eat their words, and some of them were smart enough to also eat a lot of sockeye salmon whose biting habits *were* discovered.

Fly fishermen and spinning rod users carried back to the "lower 48" some tales of 50 to 80 fish days of catching sockeye on pink and red yarn ties on the Iliamna River in Alaska. At nearly the same time, Kenai River salmon anglers said that, when fishing for heavyweight chinook salmon was slow or dormant, they sometimes filled in the lonesome hours catching 30 to 40 sockeye a day, per rod, tossing small nickel or brass spinners or spoons to these sporty little salmon.

British Columbia salmon anglers of the 1960s and 1970s also trolled sheltered waters between and around the scattered islands from Vancouver Island north and into inlets of the mainland, happily hooking wads of sockeye on dodgers trailed by pink or red artificial squid or hoochies.

So, a small group of about three dozen 1970 Washington salmon anglers began fishing for the big run of sockeye salmon that entered Lake Washington past the skyscrapers of Seattle and swam south to the Cedar River, their spawning stream. What would make these fish strike? In the next two years, they found squid imitations delivered a few fish and yarn ties fewer still, while spinners and spoons were almost totally ignored!

But (and isn't it wonderful that there's always a "but"), sockeye *would* strike, chew, mangle and generally try to eliminate from the "artificial lure gene pool" a particular few banana-shaped red or bright orange plugs previously fished for bass. And, the same plankton eaters would pound these plugs in blue scale, gold and silver finish, too, as well as redheaded nickel plugs and "clown suit" patterns of vertical half-and-half nickel and red. They liked all these wobbling plugs best when they were trolled *very* slowly behind an undulating dodger trundled beside or over the sockeye schools.

Anglers assail sockeye schools in gray light from 30 feet to 50 feet below the huge lake's surface. As the sun rises, trolling gear is gradually lowered to as much as 140 feet deep to follow the sockeye. Most Lake Washington sockeye weigh 3 to 5 pounds, but some well-fed fish have been 10 pounds or more.

Sockeye began hitting so well for Lake Washington anglers that, in a few short years, anglers could catch between 15,000 and 25,000 fish in an average season, while Indian tribal nets also collected a comparable number. Today's fishery splits any substantial surplus over the 350,000 sockeye salmon needed for reproduction of the run into equal parts for sport anglers and Indian netters.

Opening of a sockeye season on Lake Washington is only by emergency declaration when and if sockeye swimming through the Hiram Chittendon Locks substantially pass the magic figure.

Big glass windows of the locks are scanned by official state department fish counters and even more longingly by avid, area anglers. In late June, if the numbers look good, sockeye-fishing fever really takes hold. Up to 5,000 boats hit the big lake per weekend day when the mid-July or early-August opening occurs. Generally, it takes five to eight weeks to catch the allowable sport bag.

More sockeye secrets crept out during the last three seasons held on Lake Washington. It seems this once-reluctant biter also can be seduced by a small dodger/tiny nickel trolling spoon rig, especially if the spoon is decorated with fire red, neon green or blue reflective tape on its upper face. And, during the last season, scads of sockeye were suckered by bare hooks!

Believe it, oldtimer ... those "non-biting" sockeye will slurp an enameled green or red 1/0 to 3/0 hook fished 10 to 12 inches behind a No. 00 dodger. No bait, no juice and no kiddin', they will eat just that bare hook.

Tailraces Can Be Terrific

Salmon fishermen should never overlook tailraces below large reservoirs for some hot fishing in summer and early fall. Almost invariably, escapees from the reservoir or salmon from downstream impoundments discover the ground-up food bonanza issuing from a dam's turbines and gorge themselves into fat and sassy football shape.

These avid eaters probe boils and currents below dams to grab tidbits from the currents. Anglers casting large spinners, plugs, spoons and other lures into the turbulent waters often can sock it to these gourmandizing salmon.

On the Cowlitz River (Washington) below the salmon hatchery barrier dam at Salkum, one special rig held terrific appeal over several years for huge fall coho runs. A No. 1 nickel spinner was a killer lure, but couldn't be cast far because of its light weight. Pinching on a No. 4 or No. 6 split shot 18 inches up the line above the spinner speedily solved that problem. It cast like a flywheel escaping its axle but, fished upstream at 30 to 45 degrees from the bank, and then allowed to hang near shore below the angler's position, paid handsome salmon dividends.

Below the upper two dams on the Missouri River, Sakakawea in North Dakota and Oahe in South Dakota, shoreline anglers use a "doctored" minnow-like plug to imitate an injured baitfish whacked by a turbine blade.

"These fishermen drill a hole through the plug's upper back, stuff a .22 short's lead in the hole, then smooth the lead flush with the plug's sides," said Pierre, South Dakota, guide Bruce Lyon. "They catch some nice fish," he said.

On a dead drift, mixmaster currents of the released Missouri River kick the weighted plug around like an injured baitfish and skillful anglers can impart struggling action to the lure with a

Tailrace 'Crippled' Plug

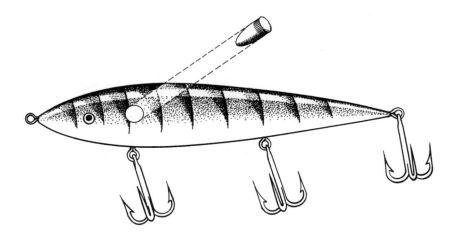

Here's how anglers fishing the Missouri River reservoirs make a "crippled" plug that will imitate the actions of baitfish chewed by the dams' turbines.

reel, stop, reel, stop retrieve. WHAM! SALMON!

Reservoir Chinooks

Chinook and coho salmon are the two species most commonly stocked in West Coast reservoirs and lakes, although sockeye also are found in lower Columbia River pools above dams and in some feeder lakes. Western salmon anglers fishing these waters generally find best success trolling for scattered schools of these transplanted sportfish. Depth locators or "fishfinders" are essential to make consistent salmon catches.

It is critical to find the year class of salmon nearest maturity and therefore the largest in size. A rule of thumb in reservoir fishing for salmon is to "look for loners" that hang below and off to sides of bait schools. A handful of large "marks" is more indicative of big salmon than a cloud of fish echoes below the same baitfish. Often, these big salmon are depicted as a string of individual blips, arrows or fish shapes cruising in a steady line at 45, 60 or 85 feet deep, separated by 10 to 20 feet on your graph or screen.

Points, bottom spikes or drop-offs, bases of river mouth deltas, deep holes and along dam faces draw reservoir salmon, especially where there is some current to disorient baitfish passing these spots. Salmon lurk behind and below obstructions and seize baitfish spilling over and past the changes in bottom. Deep weedbeds that shelter an abundant number of baitfish also yield good salmon fishing on fringes and over the weed tops.

Depending on their depth, two major methods of trolling pay off with good reservoir salmon angling for persistent anglers. Shallow waters—50 to 100 feet—yield excellent fishing to trolled crescent sinker, dodger and plastic squid/spoon/plug users. A prime example of this is Lake Wenatchee, in eastern Washington, where the hottest sockeye combination is 3 to 5 ounces of salmon sinker weight, a No. 00 chrome dodger with blue scale reflective tape and a 4-inch, flattened-banana-shape, fire-orange plug.

Downriggers are generally used in lakes and reservoirs deeper than 100 feet. They better control depths at which attractors and lures are trolled. For instance, in Lake Chelan, Washington and Coeur d'Alene Lake, Idaho, boaters rig with No. 00 to 1 dodgers and plastic squid or minnow-imitating plugs, towing them 45 to 130 feet deep behind downrigger balls for fine salmon fishing.

Techniques For Landlocked Atlantics

During spring and fall, when landlocked salmon run the tributaries of major bodies of water—for instance, the Bouquet, Saranac and Lamoille Rivers of Lake Champlain—fly fishing, using techniques developed by trout fishermen, can be highly productive. In the lower pools, close to the mouth of these rivers, the fish readily take various flies.

Streamers are most commonly used to tempt spring-run landlocked salmon which follow the schools of spawning smelt into the shallows at this time. However, rather than actually lurk in the pools, the salmon come into the river on feeding

This 10-pound, 4-ounce Atlantic salmon fell victim to a white-trimmed-with-blue-tape North Port Nailer. NAFC Member Jeff Gottsacker caught it on a Dipsy Diver rod while trolling at a depth of 65 feet in Lake Michigan.

forays and retreat to open water; a pool can be barren of salmon one minute and then have half a dozen rampaging fish the next.

A fast retrieve is essential at this point to attract the salmon's attention since the pool is full of bait and on a regular retrieve, the streamer gets lost in the crowd. Some anglers go as far as to stick the butt section of their fly rod under their arm and strip in line with both hands. Large, bright streamers also help attract attention. A No. 2 or even 2/0 Mickey Finn will often produce good results; other times Maine streamer patterns like the Grey Ghost are effective.

Small Flies For The Fall

Fall fishing is totally different. With the first heavy rains of autumn, the salmon enter the river intent on the spawning redds upstream. Small, delicate and natural are the key words here. As is the case for anadromous Atlantic salmon, landlocks do not feed on their spawning runs, but can be tempted to take various wet flies, nymphs and even dry flies. Hendrickson nymph dressings in No. 10 through 14 are quite good in the pools themselves, though in the faster water of the runs at the head of the pools, a larger, weighted stone fly nymph should be used. The March Brown is another productive October landlocked salmon pattern.

Out on the open water of the lakes, a wobbler/minnow rig ranks high for landlocked salmon. (Be sure to check your local angling regulations to make sure that the use of baitfish is legal.) Starting with a silver wobbler about 3 inches in length, remove the treble hook and tie on an 18-inch length of monofilament, a couple of pounds lighter than the line on your reel. To this, snell a single hook, and then lip-hook a dead smelt. The rig should be trolled at a fairly fast speed and when you feel a bump, resist the temptation to set the hook. Instead, drop the rodtip and wait for the salmon to come back and pick up the bait. When it does, the fish generally hits hard and streaks off across the water—the act of setting the hook at this stage is only a token gesture.

Special Techniques—Great Lakes Salmon

Since the salmon explosion in the Great Lakes kicked off in the mid-1960s, one of the most popular periods has been the fall—when spawning Pacific salmon enter the natal tributaries where they were stocked or reproduced naturally. Huge runs of mature fish converge to potential spawning sites, hoping to add to the lake's salmon populations. When their mission is complete, they will soon die, unlike their Atlantic salmon counterpart.

When Pacific salmon are getting ready to spawn, their body undergoes a metamorphosis. Their stomachs actually start to shrink, and they no longer feed like the eating machines they were a few years prior. Because of this change, it was thought that the only way Pacific salmon could be "caught" in the fall was through snagging and snatching methods of ripping weighted treble hooks through deep holes and likely salmon-holding areas, or just off piers at river mouths when salmon start their fall migration upstream.

Since then, those early beliefs have been proven wrong by dedicated sportsmen throughout the Great Lakes Basin. These fish *will* hit lures and baits through conventional fishing methods, and many states have eliminated or severely curtailed all forms of snagging and snatching. The educational process is now underway to teach the general public how these fish act and react under certain fall-type situations and baits. It's not as easy as snagging, but the end result will be more rewarding. It always is for anything you have to work harder to get.

Spawning Pacific salmon entering Great Lakes tributaries are quite susceptible to standard angling procedures, but special care and attention needs to be given by the angler. First and foremost, you want to approach a potential pool with caution, either from boat or shore, being extremely careful not to spook the fish. Once they're spooked, they're extremely difficult to catch by any method.

One of the most popular means to entice spawning salmon to hit is through use of eggs, egg sacks or egg imitations—imitating the salmon eggs from mature female chinook and coho species. Egg sacks can be purchased at local tackle shops, or anglers can tie them. If tying your own, you can add variations such as multi-colored styrofoam balls. Not only does it have attracting qualities, but it adds buoyancy to give it a more natural presentation as the current rolls it along the bottom. The key to your success will be to create as natural a presentation as possible in areas that hold fish.

Good salmon holding areas include undercut banks, pocket pools, behind rocks and boulders, along eddies, behind stumps and logs, as well as abutments from bridges—even below waterfalls or dams, the first impassible barrier for these traveling fish.

Using big clumps of treated egg skein still in the membrane, (see section on pier fishing for recipe and further explanation) river anglers will drift a three-way rig. This method, which incorporates the use of a three-way swivel, is very effective on spawning fall fish. One eye of the swivel is tied to the main line of 15- to 20-pound test. The trailing eye will sport a 12- to 14-pound test leader, which is usually about the length of your rod, or a little less. This is what your hook or bait will be

This pool along rock ledges has become a resting area for nearly a dozen salmon as they make their way back upstream in the fall. The salmon can be seen through the middle of the picture, almost in a line.

attached to. In the Niagara River, early season tactics include drifting banana baits this way until salmon are of sufficient numbers to use eggs.

Off the bottom eye, at the end of an 8- to 12-inch leader of 8- to 10-pound-test line, will be a slinky weight just touching bottom, not dragging severely. When using eggs, try and fish the drift as slow as possible, using an electric trolling motor to slow you down. Fish the eggs underneath the boat. If your weight gets hung up, you'll lose the weight—not the lure or bait. It also allows you to get back in the water much quicker.

For shallower rivers, MacKenzie River-type drift boats (about 16 to 17 feet long with an upswept bow and stern, no keel) are used in order to maneuver in the rivers like salmon. Bob Jordan, a local river guide, will use this method to back into salmon-holding areas with eggs, flies, artificial eggs and wobbling plugs—whatever the fish want. Hot Shots are popular plugs for this fishing method throughout the Great Lakes, but they certainly don't have the market concerned. One of the things that Jordan does is paint the tips of his rods a bright chartreuse to make it easier for the customers to see when a fish is hitting.

"Concentrate on the drift," says Jordan. "When you see something inconsistent with the normal action of the drift, set the hook." He also uses Berkley Trilene Solar line for his main monofilament to help increase visibility—especially under low-light conditions. He still uses a clear leader, however.

Casting from shore or boats can also entail any of the methods listed earlier for pier fishing. Heavy spoons worked along the bottom are always popular, as are spinners and short wobbling body baits. Some bass favorites, such as rattle lures, do an excellent job angering salmon into hitting out of aggression.

In recent years, boats anchoring just inside river mouths in bays and harbors have done well casting various plugs, including stickbaits.

There are often conflicts between boat and shore fishermen that shouldn't exist. Show common courtesy when encountering a fellow angler, and treat them as you would want to be treated. Also be sure to respect landowner rights and never litter. If you see a violation of the fish and game laws, write down all the details you can and contact a local conservation officer as soon as possible. It's up to the sportsmen to protect their own resources. Every illegal act is taking something away from you and me.

Terminal Tackle Knots

The Uni-Knot System

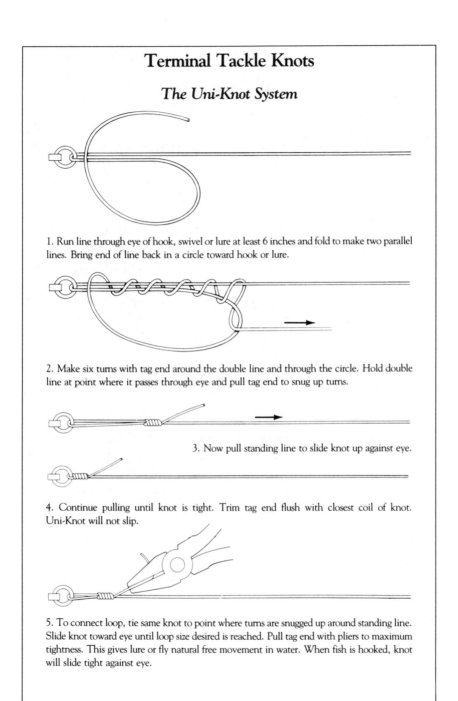

1. Run line through eye of hook, swivel or lure at least 6 inches and fold to make two parallel lines. Bring end of line back in a circle toward hook or lure.

2. Make six turns with tag end around the double line and through the circle. Hold double line at point where it passes through eye and pull tag end to snug up turns.

3. Now pull standing line to slide knot up against eye.

4. Continue pulling until knot is tight. Trim tag end flush with closest coil of knot. Uni-Knot will not slip.

5. To connect loop, tie same knot to point where turns are snugged up around standing line. Slide knot toward eye until loop size desired is reached. Pull tag end with pliers to maximum tightness. This gives lure or fly natural free movement in water. When fish is hooked, knot will slide tight against eye.

Terminal Tackle Knots

Improved Clinch Knot

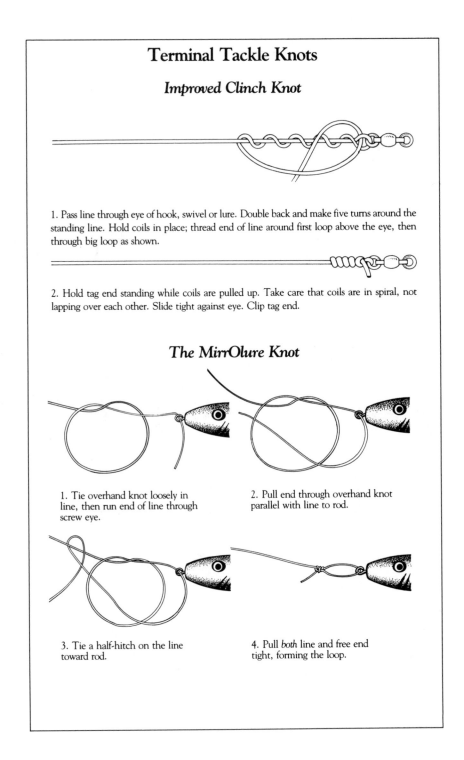

1. Pass line through eye of hook, swivel or lure. Double back and make five turns around the standing line. Hold coils in place; thread end of line around first loop above the eye, then through big loop as shown.

2. Hold tag end standing while coils are pulled up. Take care that coils are in spiral, not lapping over each other. Slide tight against eye. Clip tag end.

The MirrOlure Knot

1. Tie overhand knot loosely in line, then run end of line through screw eye.

2. Pull end through overhand knot parallel with line to rod.

3. Tie a half-hitch on the line toward rod.

4. Pull *both* line and free end tight, forming the loop.

Index

weight, 44, 49
world record, 46, 49

B

Back-bouncing technique, 170-171
Bait canteens, 73
Baitcasting reels, 61
Baitcasting rods, 71
Ball sinkers, 112
Blackmouth, 31, 32
Bluebacks, 36
Boat rods, 64
Boats, 86-89, 175
Boondogging, 172
Brake system, 66
Break walls, 219-220
Bucktail, 70, 126

C

Caddis flies, 138
Calico salmon, 39
Canadian Shield, 48
Candlefish, 35
Canoes, 184-185
Caplin, 43
Casting, 70
Caudal fin, 34
Center downriggers, 110
Centre-pin, 62
Chinook salmon, 18-19, 21, 25, 31-34,
  164-172
    color, 18, 32-33
    habitat, 32
    kype, 32
    life cycle, 33-34
    world record, 32
Chum salmon, 39, 174-175
Calico salmon, 39
Color, 39
    dog salmon, 39
    habitat, 39, 175
    kype, 39
    range, 39
Cluster eggs, 153-154, 173
Coeur d'Alene, 25
Coho salmon, 19-20, 21, 26, 31, 34-35,
  172-174
    color, 19, 34
    eyesight, 35
    food, 35
    habitat, 35, 172
    hearing, 35

hooknose, 34
kype, 34
range, 35
size, 19, 34
silver salmon, 34, 172-174
spawning, 35, 172
world record, 19
Corner downriggers, 110
Counting out, 215-216
Crabs, 142
Crankbaits, 138
Crayfish, 138, 149
Crustaceans, 43

D

Daily limits, 193
Deck shoes, 72
Deep jigging, 224-228
Deep jigging rods, 228
Depthfinders, 78-82, 229, 237
Diploid-type salmon, 19
Dipsy-diver rods, 59
Divers, 70, 90-94
Dodgers, 26, 96-98, 124, 137, 202
Dog salmon, 39
Downrigger reels, 58-59
Downrigger rods, 56-59
Downriggers, 26, 56-59, 70, 108-115, 123,
  137, 195
Drag, 58, 61, 62, 64, 67
Drift bobbers, 130
Drift rigs, 127, 148, 149, 168, 172, 178
Drift bobbers, 130, 149
Drift fishing, 61, 178
Drift-fishing rods, 61
Drop-back technique, 170-171
Dry flies, 126, 138-141, 187-192

E

Egg clusters, 150
Egg skeins, 150-151
El Vado Reservoir, 27

F

Fairhaven, 21
Feeding grounds, 43, 44
Fiberglass rods, 58
Files, 73
Fingerlings, 34, 43
Fishing diary, 200
Flashers, 26, 96-98, 124, 137
Flashers (depthfinders), 78

249